A BOOK FOR BOSTON

JUBILEE 350

A BOOK FOR BOSTON

IN WHICH ARE GATHERED ESSAYS, STORIES,

AND POEMS BY DIVERS HANDS

ESPECIALLY WRITTEN IN HONOR OF THE

CITY UPON THE OCCASION OF THE THREE

HUNDRED AND FIFTIETH ANNIVERSARY OF

ITS INCORPORATION THE TWENTIETH DAY

OF SEPTEMBER ANNO DOMINI

SIXTEEN HUNDRED AND THIRTY

David R. Godine, Publisher

Boston City Hall, designed by Kallmann, McKinnell & Knowles and built in 1968. Photograph by Cervan Robinson.
THE BOSTON SOCIETY OF ARCHITECTS

FRONTISPIECE: "A North East View of the Great Town of Boston," attributed to William Burgis, 1723. BOSTON PUBLIC LIBRARY

May 14, 1980

To All Friends of Boston:

Throughout her long history, Boston has always been a happy marriage of ideas and expressions. From our first days on the map, Bostonians have been defining themselves through the written word.

The world has turned over many times since Cotton Mather, our first great author, held sway, but the literary aspirations of this City have forever kept pace with her sense of destiny. In the nineteenth century, we were the "Athens of America," and our Parnassus, the handsome brick structure at the corner of School and Washington Streets. At the Old Corner Book Store congregated the heroes of American letters, Hawthorne and Emerson, Alcott and Longfellow, and in among its well-stocked bookshelves was born the Golden Age of American literature.

Only ghosts review the latest publications at School and Washington today, but the genius of Boston for expressing moral and philosophical convictions has never left its residents.

I grew up with books, in a home where the written word vied with political involvement as the highest form of self-expression. Like so many Boston parents from the days of Anne Bradstreet to the present, my mother had a love of books that was fierce and infectious. And like so many other kids from all of Boston's neighborhoods, I was taught at an early age to use and enjoy the Boston Public Library—an institution which we can all proudly claim as an essential part of Boston's intellectual heritage.

As I walk around Boston today, I find abundant evidence that books play as big a role in the life of Boston as they did when J. P. Marquand held forth at the Somerset Club and Edwin O'Connor could be found each noon at the Ritz.

From the Beacon Hill of James Carroll and Robin Cook to the Dorchester of Teddy White, Boston is still a city in love with the printed page. The flow of information and ideas from Boston's great universities and publishing houses continues unabated after 350 years. And if few Bostonians nowadays would willingly sit down with a Mather treatise on original sin, many of us would be pleased to debate its conclusions.

During this, Boston's 350th birthday year, it is good to remember our glorious past. But a city that lives in the past is ill-prepared for the future. If the stories, poems, and essays that follow are any indication, Boston's literary future is secure. I hope you will enjoy reading A Book for Boston as much as I have.

Sincerely,

Kevin H. White
Mayor

Staffordshire plate showing the State House and Boston Common in the foreground, 1805. BOSTON ATHENAEUM.

First published in 1980 by

David R. Godine, Publisher, Inc.
306 Dartmouth Street
Boston, Massachusetts 02116

LC 79–55279
ISBN 0–87923–317–6 (hardcover)
ISBN 0–87923–321–4 (softcover)

Manufactured in the United States of America

Contents

Message from the Mayor   v

Editor's Preface   1

THOMAS SAVAGE   Why a Pilgrim Traveled to Boston,
   and His Implausible Arrival There   13

FELICIA LAMPORT   Overdrivers   22

JANE HOLTZ KAY   The Walking City   27

FELICIA LAMPORT   Academic Asset   36

NANCY HALE   "Who Needs No Introduction . . ."   39

ALAN LUPO   This Is What Politics Is   47

FELICIA LAMPORT   Means Test   62

ANNE BERNAYS   Cambridge 02138   65

JUSTIN KAPLAN   The Party of the Present   71

JAMES ALAN MCPHERSON   One in the Sun, Joe   77

JOHN D. SPOONER   A Sure Thing on State Street   99

JAMES CARROLL   Fireflies   105

JOSEPH E. GARLAND   The Doctors' City   123

CARYL RIVERS   The Battle of Maverick Street   135

FELICIA LAMPORT   Minority Priority   144

ROBERT B. PARKER   Childhood's Song   151

FELICIA LAMPORT   Garden Variety   156

JOHN KENNETH GALBRAITH   The Quite Elegant Future of Boston   159

DAVID MCCORD   Poem for the Occasion   167
   with a foreword by ARCHIBALD MACLEISH

JULIA CHILD and E. S. YNTEMA   A Boston Birthday Buffet   187

FELICIA LAMPORT   High Rationale   200

ELIZABETH SAVAGE   Bringing George Home   207

The Contributors   214

Painting of Increase Mather by John Vanderspriet, London, 1688.
MASSACHUSETTS HISTORICAL SOCIETY

Editor's Preface

I

A BOOK FOR BOSTON is, I am cheerfully perplexed to report, both more and less than its title suggests. It is more because the contributors to it are men and women of exceptional talent from many different backgrounds and with many—and sometimes surprisingly—different points of view. It is less because it proves that no single book can begin to convey the full range of aptitudes, attitudes, and moral and intellectual altitudes that for 350 years have given Boston its unique place in the life of the New World—and the Old.

If A Book for Boston had been written by committee and with strict regard for the current demographics of Boston, it would, I know, have been a more balanced book. (At least it would have been an easier book to explain.) But I am not persuaded that it would have been a better book, any more than I am persuaded that Boston Common would be a better green space if its paths were more logically laid out, its trees more symmetrically arranged, its functions more clearly defined.

My perplexity about what this book is or ought to be does not end with the contents of A Book for Boston, either. Ponder the occasion for its publication: Boston's seventh jubilee.

The jubilee tradition is long established here in Boston. Ever since 1730 the city has faithfully observed each fifty-year anniversary of its incorporation, in September 1630. Lengthy sermons were the principal form of observance in colonial Boston. But by 1880, Boston's fourth jubilee, the celebration had developed into a full-scale birthday party, complete with parades, patriotic orations, crying toddlers, band concerts, and a brisker than usual business for the gin mills of the town. The Great Depression and that other national disaster Prohibition had no apparent impact on Boston's fifth jubilee, in 1930—a summer-long carnival that ended with an eight-hour parade, complete with 108 marching units, 200 floats, and 40,000 footsore marchers. Upwards of a million people lined the streets to cheer the procession on. Many who were present then will be on hand (and foot) to celebrate Jubilee 350, which promises to be the biggest bash of all.

But, as I say, I am puzzled. For I find that the term *jubilee* has been rather loosely construed in recent centuries. Even its derivation is not what one might expect. *Jubilum* is a Latin noun of ancient and impeccable Greek ancestry: it means "a shout" or "a shout for joy"; it is the root of the English noun *jubilation*—"a triumphant shouting." The English noun *jubilee*, on the other hand—"an anniversary celebration"—derives from the Hebrew *jūbāl* (after Jūbāl, the musical son of Lamech), meaning "ram's horn." To the extent that the sounding of a ram's horn and the shouting of many voices signal joyful times, a jubilee must be considered a jubilant occasion. But it is nowhere written in the Old Testament that the sounding of the *jūbāl* is an invitation to a toga party.

Indeed, the jubilee so carefully described in the Book of Leviticus (28:8–55) was apparently a temporary response to a unique set of social, religious, and political imperatives during the early history of the postexilic Jews. It marked a singular year following every forty-ninth (or seven times seven "Sabbath" years), when all debts were ordered forgiven, when all alienated property was to be returned to its original owners, and when the sowing and reaping of all crops were strictly forbidden. The Jewish debtor, landlord, and slave or bond servant would have had every reason to be jubilant when the *jūbāl* was heard in the land. But the Old Testament jubilee was primarily a device—even a coercive device—for national survival. It signaled the return to the status quo, the restoration of order to a people on the brink of dispersal.

The last formal Jewish jubilee fell in the first century A.D. But when, in 1300, a variant of the jubilee first entered the Christian calendar, much of the original ambiguity remained. At intervals of a hundred, then fifty, and, since the fifteenth century, twenty-five years, the Church of Rome has regularly declared holy years. These jubilees not only affirm the primacy and majesty of the Church, they also serve to bind together the far-flung Christian community. This, too, must be said about the Roman Catholic jubilee tradition: it is by no means always a time for rejoicing. Popes have often declared special or extraordinary jubilees when the welfare of the Church or of a Christian state is threatened. Wars, plagues, famines, and revolutions—not just happy anniversaries—are a vital part of the jubilee heritage. Between survival and celebration, survival has always had the inside track.

Where does this leave Boston and Jubilee 350?

It is fair to assume that the Bay Colony's Puritan divines had read and pondered Lev. 28:8–55 even before the incorporation of Boston 350 years ago. They must also have been keenly aware that the Church of Rome was in the jubilee business. How the early Puritans interpreted all this is open to reasonable discussion. What is incontrovertible is that the survival of Boston during its first fifty years, never mind its first 350 years, has had a tremendous impact on the course of Western history. The seed planted in the rocky soil of Massachusetts has rooted most amazingly. Through good times and bad, through wars, plagues, famines, and revolutions, Boston has held firm and led the way.

Boston's Jubilee 350 is, thus, neither a strictly secular occasion nor, strictly, a religious one. It is neither a time for uncritical self-congratulation nor a time for bitter self-reproach.

Boston's Jubilee 350 is, rather, an occasion for thanksgiving. It is a time to forgive, when that is possible, or to forbear when it is not.

Above all, Boston's Jubilee 350 is a time for self-renewal and rededication. It is—as I hope all future Boston jubilees will be—that singular year in each fifty years when prospect and retrospect are one.

II

The genesis of *A Book for Boston* was Deputy Mayor Katharine D. Kane's conviction that Jubilee 350 was a milestone worthy of a book. Boston stockbroker-novelist John D. Spooner shared Kathy Kane's conviction, and he suggested that the book be a gathering of original pieces about the city by prominent writers identified with Boston. The Jubilee organization agreed to

HOWLAND Editor's Preface　　3

fund honoraria for the contributing authors. Isabelle Storey, as picture editor, and I, as textual editor, gratefully accepted this Jubilee group's invitation to help turn an idea into an actuality. And David R. Godine—a brave fellow and a good friend of Boston—graciously agreed to publish the result. Howard Kaye, Jr., representing the city of Boston, endured with uncommon patience the flood of calls and correspondence the book's editors generated. John Taylor Williams, Esquire, drafted the letter agreement that bound contributors and publisher together.

From the outset it was obvious—how could it not be?—that the creation of such a book would involve working against a tight deadline and taking certain unavoidable risks and making any number of difficult and sometimes entirely arbitrary decisions. Which writers would be invited to contribute to the book? Of the writers we hoped might contribute, which would accept the invitation? Of these, which were likely to meet the deadline—never mind what the form and content of their contributions would be? For that matter, should contributors be allowed to choose their themes, or should they be urged to write more or less to order? How much should, could, the Boston Foundation offer contributors, and should these amounts be open to negotiation? The list goes on.

Some of the questions were and must forever remain unanswerable. The answers to others can easily be inferred from the roster of contributors to *A Book for Boston*—and what they wrote about. Nevertheless, readers deserve to know the editorial ground rules, as Isabelle Storey and I—and anyone else involved—attempted to spell them out:

—The initial qualification was that a contributor be identified with Boston "by birth, education, or long association." Boston was defined as metropolitan Boston—that is, most of eastern Massachusetts.

—Authors then currently on the payroll of any Boston-based magazine, newspaper, or publishing house were excluded, no matter how accomplished they might be. (The reasoning was that regularly published columnists and editors would have ample opportunity to comment on Boston's Jubilee 350 in the public prints.)

—Although we sought (and were fortunate to get) contributions from Bostonians of national celebrity, we invited only those celebrities who had demonstrated their ability to write sound English prose.

—All authors, regardless of what they could command in the literary market, were offered the same fee, with the promise of the same token bonus if they delivered before the deadline. No contributors disputed this approach, and one author even declined the honorarium (he asked that it be used by the city of Boston "for the benefit of the people of Boston"—and so it will be, and I wish he had allowed me to reveal his name, for this gesture deserves a memorial).

—Although some contributors were asked to consider writing on a particular topic, all were urged to propose a theme of their own, provided it didn't overlap territory already claimed by another.

—We asked that the prose pieces run between 1,500 and 5,000 words and that poetry be of equivalent length (whatever that means). But all contributors were encouraged to run longer, if not shorter, as inspiration dictated.

—Finally, we stipulated that all contributions be original—that we have the right to publish them in A Book for Boston before any other use was made of them. There is only one exception to this rule: David McCord's Poem for the Occasion was first written, in 1970, for the hundredth anniversary of Boston's Museum of Fine Arts and published in a limited edition of 300 copies. An exceptional poem deserves to be treated accordingly. To David McCord, and to Archibald MacLeish, who revised for our book the introduction he wrote for McCord's, all thanks and felicitations.

The Boston Foundation ultimately invited twenty-two writers to contribute to A Book for Boston. Of these, one politely but firmly declined, two declined with letters that in themselves do tribute to the citizens and the city of Boston, and a fourth dropped out only when he realized that he would risk missing the deadline by a substantial margin. The other eighteen are the authors whose work appears in the following pages.

My primary job was to solicit and edit the text contributions. On Isabelle Storey fell the responsibility for creating an evocative visual portrait of Boston, as the city has developed and been depicted down the centuries. The images she has selected (some from historical archives and private collections,

HOWLAND *Editor's Preface* 5

some specially commissioned for *A Book for Boston* and representing the work of first-rank contemporary American photographers) should be considered essays in their own right. Certainly they give a dimension to the book that the written essays cannot.

Here, then, is why and how *A Book for Boston* came to be.

III

Editors may claim to be objective judges of books that they have edited; I've yet to meet an editor who was. On the other hand, it is pretty obvious even to me that *A Book for Boston* has its share of limitations. These limitations I would divide into two classes: inherent and adherent.

A Book for Boston is inherently a flattering and partial representation of Boston past and present. Like the gnomon in *The Christian Science Monitor*— itself one of the countless Boston institutions that get scant or no attention in this book—the essays by and large record "only sunny hours."

From *A Book for Boston* readers will gain no special insight into the social and economic woes—including the curse of racism—that still plague our city (but which cannot be said to be unique to Boston). When it comes to crime and corruption, death and taxes, *A Book for Boston* looks the other way.

Readers may well grow irritated at the number of references to Harvard University, Beacon Hill, Faneuil Hall, the Old State House. Well they might ask, And what of Charlestown and Hyde Park, Columbia Point and Codman Square?

Another inherent limitation of *A Book for Boston* is the unequal treatment accorded even those institutions and aspects of Boston that are, by common consent, the chief wonders of the city. Four hundred lines on the Museum of Fine Arts; barely a mention of the Boston Symphony (or Seiji Ozawa), the Boston Pops (or the late cantankerous and beloved Arthur Fiedler), the Opera Company of Boston (or the incomparable Sarah Caldwell), or Elma Lewis (who is an institution more durable than adamant). A long, vital essay on Boston's political traditions, but only an occasional aside about that complex, immensely powerful force Max Weber called the "Protestant Ethic," which the Jansenists in our midst compel us to rename the "Puritan Ethic." (Perhaps no concept has been so widely used with so little real understanding by so many Bostonians and students of Boston. Perhaps nothing better explains what makes the city tick.)

At a certain point, however, the inherent limitations of *A Book for Boston* become "adherent" limitations; and at this point, I believe, the limitations may properly be regarded as strengths. For the fact is, Boston contains multitudes. The fact is, it is a city that generates passionate loyalties and passionate enmities, but a city whose stability and greatness depend largely on the constant interplay of opposing viewpoints.

Eighteen of Boston's most prominent writers, having been invited to pay tribute to Boston during Jubilee 350, have accepted the invitation. Adhering to a time-honored Boston tradition, they have written what it pleased them to write, about that which it pleased them to write about. Their Boston may not be your Boston. It may not be my Boston. A writer's Boston it certainly is. As editor of this book, I could not have asked for more from the contributors. I would not have settled for less.

Llewellyn Howland III
Jamaica Plain

Ship carver's sign (probably made for Samuel L. Winsor), owned by McIntire & Gleason, later by Hastings & Gleason. THE BOSTONIAN SOCIETY

"S.E. Prospect from an Eminence near the Common, Boston," lithograph drawn and engraved by S. Hall, 1790. BOSTON ATHENAEUM

8 A BOOK FOR BOSTON

"A Prospective View of part of the Commons," engraved by Sidney L. Smith after a 1768 watercolor by Christian Remick. BOSTON ATHENAEUM

Old Elm on Boston Common. WIDENER LIBRARY, HARVARD UNIVERSITY

OPPOSITE: *"The Race," Boston Public Garden, ca. 1907.*
SOCIETY FOR THE PRESERVATION OF NEW ENGLAND ANTIQUITIES

The Race
Public Garden

THOMAS SAVAGE

Why a Pilgrim Traveled to Boston, and His Implausible Arrival There

I first heard of Boston from the Sheep Queen of Idaho, who was my grand-mother. She sat at the dining-room table in what the hired men called the Big House, because it was big, and there important things were said about Duty and Loyalty and Compassion and Early Rising. We all knew what happened to Late Risers. Nothing. Nobody ate at the Big House except on holidays and birthdays, when the whole Family came from all over and my grand-mother pretended they didn't bring gin and whiskey with them and that the girls didn't smoke. (For all other meals everybody ate down at the cookhouse by the creek, and my grandmother sat at the head of that table and her fore-man sat at the foot, where she could speak directly to him over the boiled mutton, boiled beet greens, and boiled beans.)

The table in the Big House where nobody often ate was piled with old copies of *The Salt Lake Tribune* and the *Idaho Statesman* that might have something in them she'd missed, and the *National Woolgrowers Magazine*, with pictures of famous sheep. My grandmother's check-writing machine looked like a small cash register; it was black and shiny and so was her Water-man's fountain pen. It would have been crazy to try to forge her signature.

Every year on an evening early in June, when it was still cold when the sun set behind the mountains up Hayden Creek, the ten men of the shearing crew arrived with their bedrolls in old Fords and Overlands. Aside from their wages, my grandmother supplied their food, the tents they slept in, and hay for their mattresses. She walked out with her dog to greet them; she respected

OPPOSITE: *Union Club, built in 1805 on Park Street.*
Photograph by J. W. Black, June 17, 1875. BOSTON PUBLIC LIBRARY

their skill and she addressed them as Mr. Hawkins, Mr. Hoffman, and Mr. Rameriz—she needed them as much as they needed her. She asked after their wives and children, whose names she remembered. She walked out to them in a long, faded old red wool coat her daughters wished she'd get rid of, and she carried a long forked stick she used to pin down rattlesnakes before she crushed their heads under her heavy, wide shoes. Her voice carried, and her laughter. The shearers knew when they got into trouble they had only to telephone or write and everything would be fine.

"It's just wonderful how Mama gets along with all sorts of people," my mother said. When later on my grandmother went to Europe, she got along with Ambassador Dawes in Germany and with the Pope in Rome.

In the morning when the mountain sun had scorched the dew off the sheeps' backs, shearing began. The shearing shed was a long, low building of rough lumber with a canvas roof fitted over the rafters. Along each side were little pens for a few sheep that were replaced and replaced from outside. Articulated shafts—arm, elbow, and forearm that terminated in clippers like those in barber shops—depended from an overhead shaft powered by a one-lung gasoline engine; the explosive exhaust crashed against the slide-rock hill where the Indians used to bury their dead. A shearer grabbed a sheep by the hind leg and threw her on her back. Shocked, she lay passive.

Zip-zip-zip. A good shearer took no more than eight minutes to fleece a sheep and the wool was all of a piece, like a carefully peeled orange. Outside the shed a gibbet was set up like that used to hang a man. Where a man might be dropped through, the fleece tied with twine was tossed and it dropped down into a woolsack suspended beneath the opening. From time to time a man crawled up and tramped new fleeces into a compact mass, and when the sack was stuffed full with the wool of some fifty sheep, he cut it down from the gibbet and sewed up the end with a big needle, sharp and curved like an eagle's claw.

A full woolsack is impressive. Three feet by seven, it weighs between two hundred and fifty and four hundred pounds, depending on the amount of oil in the wool, and I was not surprised later to find that the Lord Chancellor sits on a woolsack in the House of Lords—not only, I think, because a sack of wool is a symbol of the British economy but also because wool is basic to human comfort. Wool is essential, like fire. It keeps you warm.

At last more than two hundred sacks were neatly piled up like huge cordwood on a wooden platform—a mountain of wool. I was seven years old, and when I climbed up there I was higher than anybody and nothing could get me. I was sorry to see the mountain hauled off on trucks.

"Where does it go?" I asked my grandmother that night in the formal dining room.

From the cluttered table she looked out the window over the potted geraniums at the trucks moving up the grade to the railroad, but with no sense of loss. Departing wool had made possible college educations, three meals a day for everybody, clothes, and a stone house with extra rooms where everybody was safe.

"It goes to big brick warehouses with very few windows. It goes to Boston. I talked there once at a convention and stayed in a hotel named the Copley Plaza."

"Where is Boston?"

"Back East. Back of the mountains, beside the sea."

My grandmother had a hand in Boston. We all had.

During the next fifteen years, hints of Boston turned up like signs along a highway. In grammar school around Thanksgiving I cut out gray-and-brown Pilgrims who had once hunted wild turkeys around Boston with muskets whose barrels terminated in bells, like a trumpet's. The history books in high school had drawings of Paul Revere's house, and Faneuil Hall.

"One if by land," Miss Anderson cried, "two if by sea!" She turned to stare out the window, where in the middle of the lawn the American flag struggled against its moorings. "Two if by sea. And I on the opposite shore will be!" In her dress ties she looked every inch her five foot two. She drove one of the earliest Plymouths, which had Floating Power.

Miss Eastman taught English and drama and was suspect for her big hats, her chiffon scarves, and her hateful aplomb. Her weekend trips went noticed but unexplained; she had reportedly been seen smoking cigarettes with well-dressed strangers in hotel dining rooms throughout the state. She was said to have been seen reading Communist tracts, but in class she championed the New England classics. She was tall; she extended her long arm, pointed her finger at the corner of the room, and sighted along it. " 'Build thee more stately mansions,' " she commanded. " 'O my soul, As the swift seasons roll! Leave thy low-vaulted past! Let each new temple, nobler than the last, Shut thee from heaven with a dome more vast, Till thou at length art free, Leaving thine outgrown shell by life's unresting sea!' Ah Holmes! Ah Lowell! Ah Emerson, Thoreau, and Bryant! Small wonder they call Boston the Athens of America!"

I wrote my name on the flyleaf of my text and after it I wrote "Boston," to see how it would look.

I spent a year at the University of Montana in Missoula. I wanted to be a writer and thought I might be a better writer somewhere else; the Rocky Mountains were too familiar and everybody talked the same. In high school Miss Schoenborn had taught me Spanish well and I talked it with Mexican sheepherders and Mexican section hands in pool halls and with the night telegrapher down at the Union Pacific depot; at three in the morning he made coffee on a hot plate kept hidden away from the Officials. He had lived in Mexico. Why not go to the National University in Mexico City? I thought that anybody who knew that in Spanish there are two forms of the past subjunctive couldn't go far wrong in Mexico.

"When I was in high school here," a nice local girl in Missoula said, "my best friend was as crazy about writing as you are."

I thought that unlikely. I'd had an article published in *Coronet* about how to break a horse. They gave me seventy-five dollars and I invested half of it in gold stock that failed.

"Her father is a writer in places like *Collier's* and *The Saturday Evening Post*. He taught writing here at the University before they went away."

"Where did they go?"

"Back to where they came from. Back around Boston. She's good-looking and I think she's unhappy. Now she goes to some little college back there that nobody ever heard of."

"Why do you think she's unhappy?"

"It's hard to say, but if people are like anybody else they don't have to write. They're happy the way they are and don't have to make things up. She won a contest."

"And yet you say she's unhappy."

It is—or was—ninety-six hours by bus from Butte, Montana, to Boston, Massachusetts. I had once read that some scientists got hold of some dogs—beagles, I'm afraid—and kept them awake until they died, and it wasn't much more than ninety-six hours, either. When you cross the Red River between Fargo, North Dakota, and Moorhead, Minnesota, the West is behind you, and you may never be the same again. Euclid is the stylish avenue in Cleveland. Lake Erie is flat and gray and cold like lead.

I recognized the girl because she'd sent me her picture. I said, "Aren't you the one I'm looking for?"

"I think I am."

She and her mother both wore hats and high-heeled shoes.

"Well, there's always the Merry-Go-Round at the Copley Plaza," the mother said.

The girl looked at me. "You're sure you're not too tired?"

The Copley Plaza was quite as grand as my grandmother had said—crystal and marble and gilt and brocade and chairs like thrones and in the bar a round platform that slowly turned as you drank. Drinkers who preferred not to move sat at tables along the windows and along the wall. I sensed their superiority over those who must have a constantly altered view. I was not much used to drinking in those days and not at all on a moving platform, and I thought of those poor dogs, but I wanted to appear affluent in spite of having arrived by bus, and I urged the girl and her mother to have still another Tom Collins. The mother had slipped off one of her shoes; the girl had slipped off both of hers; I had not known this was done.

The round bar in the center of the platform was stationary and so was the bartender, except when he walked. I was sitting opposite the girl and the mother and a strange thing happened at the table behind them. The bartender stepped up on the turning platform and went to that table. In each hand he held a hollow glass snake frozen in motion. He paused, and then he

SAVAGE *Why a Pilgrim Traveled to Boston*   17

rubbed both snakes on the surface of the table. They glowed green. I was certain of it. The table had been wired with a mild electricity and the snakes were filled with neon gas. I knew because of Mr. Ogren in chemistry in Beaverhead County High School, but I didn't know whether the snakes were meant as conversation pieces or *épater la bourgeoisie*—like me.

I was about to speak of what was going on behind them but couldn't find the words to put it briefly and clearly, nor was I certain of its effect on two women whose conversation was so far removed from the fact that snakes might soon light up before them. They were speaking of a rich woman they knew who maintained that she did not, in spite of sound evidence to the contrary, have to go to the bathroom as often as your regular woman.

"Of course, she went to Wellesley," the mother said.

And then the bartender was there beside them with his snakes; he rubbed them on the table. He frowned. Nothing had happened.

He said, "I'm afraid this table's out of order."

The apology in his voice was lost on them. They had heard only the words.

The mother had apparently reached that point in her life when she would no longer be told she was out of order, and the girl had no intention of beginning to be told so. They rose as one and stepped down off the platform, and although it was moving very slowly it was, nevertheless, moving. When they had recovered something of their balance, they swept off with heads high as if the tumbrel awaited them—the mother limping in one shoe and the girl in no shoes at all. The girl passed through the swinging door into the kitchen regions, the mother through the glass door out into the street.

I moved to follow, but hesitated. I was almost certain to be shouted at before strangers and threatened with arrest if I left even for a few moments without first paying the check, which had not yet arrived; it was possible that the bartender, long accustomed to human deceit, would look on the entire scene as a clever ploy to avoid paying. I took out my wallet and laid down a twenty-dollar bill, and stepped off the platform.

The bartender spoke. "You forgot something."

I looked at him.

"The shoes," he said. "They're going to want their shoes."

Half blinded by the sudden natural light, I stood alone in Copley Square holding three high-heeled shoes. I was responsible for two missing women; without their shoes they were helpless, marked women and vulnerable to passing comment and opinion. With a shudder of nostalgia I wondered what my grandmother would have made of it all. Which of her granite concepts, taken to heart from McGuffey's Readers, were at the root of my entangling responsibility—Duty, Compassion, Tenacity, Family, Loyalty, Temperance? Maybe all of them—except Temperance. I was not only tired, dog-tired, but hardly sober. But Family, yes. Family, certainly. Certainly because the girl and I have been married for thirty-nine years, and I will continue to be responsible for her shoes.

Lions in front of the Kensington Building, corner of Boylston and Exeter Streets; they now stand at the main entrance to the Copley Plaza Hotel. COPLEY PLAZA HOTEL

BALLARD and BULFINCH,

Beg leave to inform the PUBLIC, and particularly the LADIES and GENTLEMEN *of this Town,—*

THAT they have furnished themselves with an elegant COACH, and a handsome pair of HORSES, which they purpose shall stand in STATE-STREET and wait the commands of any person that wish to be carried to any part of the town, from seven o'Clock in the morning, untill nine at night, at the moderate price of one shilling and four pence for each passanger. The Coach is not to be detained at any place above five minutes, unless paid for. Said Coach will run after nine at night; but it is expected an allowance will be made, according to the time it is called for after that hour.— Said BALLARD and BULFINCH purpose to keep a handsome CHAISE for the above business, and at the same hours, for one shilling each passenger; both carriages to be drove by approved drivers.

HORSES and CARRIAGES of all sorts to be let by said BALLARD, at his house in *Bromfield's-Lane.* Very easy-going HORSES, furnish'd for LADIES. CHAISES and SULKEYS without HORSES.— HORSES taken in at Livery on the most reasonable terms.

☞ LETTERS carried to any part of the Continent, on moderate Terms.

View of Bromfield Place from Mr. Ballard's establishment by Robert Salmon, 1829.
PRIVATE COLLECTION

OPPOSITE: Ballard and Bulfinch advertisement for horses and carriages in the
Continental Journal, Boston, May 12, 1785. PRIVATE COLLECTION

Overdrivers

Since Paul Revere went whizzing on his mission
   (A matter with which Longfellow has dealt)
The Boston driver's been, by long tradition,
   Intrepid as a leopard on the veldt,
      And possessor of a trenchant
      But ungovernable penchant
For distributing invective helter-skelt.

He thinks traffic lanes were put there to incite him
   And he hops them with a kangaroo's delight,
Cutting fellow-drivers off ad infinitum
   Whenever there's an inch of space in sight;
      He is singularly deft
      At signaling a left
The while he is engaged in turning right.

He sees yellow lights as urgent invitations
   To zoom through intersections unafraid
And red lights as attractive decorations
   To amuse, but surely not to be obeyed . . .
      Tourists wonder, as they cower,
      At the fender-bending power
Of the Charge of Boston's Jump-the-Light Brigade.

Scollay Square, looking toward Pemberton Square. MASSACHUSETTS HISTORICAL
SOCIETY

King's Head Tavern, ca. 1860; built in 1660 on North Street, the North End, during the reign of Charles II; taken down July 1870. MASSACHUSETTS HISTORICAL SOCIETY

Pencil drawing of shops on Hanover Street, the North End, by Charles A. Nayson.
BOSTON ATHENAEUM

The Walking City

He is, if not an apparition, then the closest thing to one that Boston possesses—so close that I do not venture near enough to count the matted gray pigtails darting from his head like a crown of thorns, or calculate how many grimy layers make up his outfit. Certainly, I do not wish to know his name or meet his eye.

Often I see him ambling around the city's best quarters, in marked contrast to the dress-for-success architecture of renewed Boston: braids bobbing, legs dangling, he is askew on the wall before the Christian Science Church Center with its flower beds and basin one day, circling the iron-gated park at the Boston Center for the Arts another, or padding leisurely around Government Center, where idling bureaucrats survey him with benign indifference.

Certainly my apparition has some notion of Boston's most seemly pedestrian environments. Obviously, too, he possesses a keen sense of survival—a well-honed notion of which neighborhoods would be generous to one of his aspect in a not always generous city. One trip through South Boston might reduce this renegade of nightmare alley to mere ash; a visit to the suburbs could bring cruise cars nipping at his heels.

Perhaps it is quixotic to trace the steps of a walking nightmare en route to tracking down what turns mere architecture into a walking city. Yet I think his habitats and his survival are pertinent. How many urban centers in America allow their picturesque, or even grotesque, citizens shelter in such pleasant and public places? How many produce such eccentrics, anyhow? Pallid cities and small towns without much color do create their characters, I admit. But prodigies like this, eccentrics who promenade along the border-

OPPOSITE: *Mt. Vernon Street, Beacon Hill, during the snow storm of 1978.*
LYNN McLAREN

line of the bizarre, do so best in surroundings that envelop them. They need a citizenry urbane enough to tolerate or enjoy the passing show. Strong surroundings allow strong characters, and Boston has its share of both.

"We all," wrote one such character, "carry the Common in our head as the unit of space, the State House as the standard of architecture, and measure off men in Edward Everetts as with a yardstick." The human yardstick has shifted since the first Oliver Wendell Holmes wrote these words, but the architectural measures remain strong. What better capsule vision for Boston than Holmes's State House, a public building still scaled to human comprehension, or his Common, a public space patterned to human movement? If a walking city sets up places for eccentrics, it must also create such architectural images for the whole citizenry. Boston has done so, I believe.

A generation ago Mary McCarthy observed that all that was truly American was invisible; that is, beyond the power of visitor or tourist to see. The American who decides to defend or describe his country, she wrote, must repudiate its visible aspect almost entirely—"He must say that its parade of phenomenology, its billboards, superhighways, even skyscrapers, not only fail to represent the inner essence of its country but in fact contravene it."

That does not hold for Boston: something of the inner essence of the city does spread before our eyes. A made city—fashioned by merchants as much as Venice, rescued from the sea as much as Holland—Boston has a landscape that not only reflects but also, literally and visibly, records the acts of its inhabitants who "cut down the hills to fill the coves." The size of the 789-acre Shawmut peninsula that the Puritan leader John Winthrop chose 350 years ago has tripled over time through such industry. Slowly, the seventeenth century's three hills, "like overtopping towers," became today's diminished Beacon and Copp's hills and the flattened environs of Fort Hill around High Street.

The quality as well as the quantity of Boston's architecture still bear witness to the heroic period of building that fashioned it. The century after 1790 transformed Beacon Hill into a compressed but still-idyllic neighborhood of bowfronted brick townhouses, filled the South End with dimmer, more brooding brick rows and parks, and finally covered the Back Bay's wetlands with a glorious parade of row houses off a new Commonwealth mall. All this is, of course, seeable, and in the walking city such arcane activity of the eyes is still best performed on foot.

Boston in its 350th birthday year remains compact enough, dense enough, and, most especially, well designed enough for the pedestrian to take in its beauties in acts of dailiness. Now, as fifty, one hundred, or one hundred and fifty years ago, a well-heeled householder can walk from the top of Beacon Hill, buy fish by the sea, and return within an hour. A trip by foot from the outer reaches of the South End to City Hall is more problematic but not much longer, while those who choose the suburbs embodied within the municipality can take the train or trolley, which, for all their foibles, have earned Boston's station-bred, tree-shrouded enclaves the label "Streetcar Suburbs."

But it is not simply the physical possibility of foot power that defines the meaning of the walking city, it seems to me. It is the nature of the architectural surroundings that invite the leisurely pace. In New York, a walk is largely a window-shopping expedition; in Chicago, unless you're an early-century skyscraper buff or choose to stroll by the river, the view is less than elevating. In Boston, the sidewalks may be bumpy but the view is lofty, an absolute orgy of fine design, a garden of green delights.

This view may be partisan but certainly no wall of luxury apartments blocks off our Charles River, a lagoon of unceasing loveliness; no threat to life and limb halts walkers from enjoying the cultivated splendors of the Public Garden. As for the architecture, the trip along the Back Bay, the classic schoolbook chronicle of passing styles—Greek to Classical Revival, with all the Victorian effusions between—finds parallels in every neighborhood and in-town quarter. In short, this pedestrian city is a city for the eyes.

Seeable, of course, does not always mean "seen." Tourists, I'm told, have a high time following the city's 5.5-mile Freedom Trail, without seeing much, however. A partly painted, partly brick stripe on the concrete sidewalk, the Trail mostly expresses a rather myopic notion of how to employ a four-man crew for six months a year in *The Last Hurrah* fashion for which the city is famous. Fixing their eyes downward guarantees that visitors will skip a lot of real nineteenth-century architecture and absorb a lot of misconceptions about the form of the eighteenth century's. The rebuilt Faneuil Hall to which we pay homage, for instance, is more than four times the size of the storybook eighteenth-century hall that "rang with patriots' cries." The Paul Revere House, also on the Trail, is distinctly the early twentieth century's work; it was then that most of the eighteenth-century addition inhabited by the Revere children was removed to "restore" the building's seventeenth-century looks.

Notwithstanding such mind-boggling myths contained in the architecture of Boston's tourism, the visitors have, however briefly, become Bostonians on one score: they have accepted the incontrovertible fact of life of the city— that it is foot-bound.

"Cars Keep Out" is, of course, the planning axiom of other would-be pedestrian cities today. Ironically, Boston planners have not recognized the value of their homegrown version half so well as some planners elsewhere. Built when all cities were perforce walking cities (with only the trolley as the essential public aid), Boston has taken its ambulatory nature for granted, or worse: too seldom have city planners made improvements on the past or adopted the pedestrian amenities installed in less congenial cities. Boston has yet to make permanent more than two auto-free enclaves or to disown the notion of in-town garages; it has yet to reinforce its crooked and narrow streets or to realize that these crabbed roadways have completed the cycle in the public's mind from antiquated to trendy. Perhaps the generation after World War II did its job too well—block that jog, straighten that curve, wipe out those last lingering ellipses, parabolas, and zigs and zags was the motto of urban renewal and the concrete mentality that created the Central Artery, the highwayesque Atlantic Avenue and Cambridge Street, and new Congress Street out of the once rambling cityscape.

Nonetheless, enough old ways do remain to recall John Winthrop's trip to the life-giving waters in the street named Spring Lane, or to recollect the graceful arch of Bulfinch's landmark Tontine Crescent rowhouses in Arch Street, and to cause back-to-the-city enthusiasts to insist that "Everything is on foot!" The printer on the side street where no car can penetrate, the grimy alleys that serve as shortcuts, the out-of-the-way tailor or bookstore survive.

Buying in Boston has rarely been a straight-line, single-minded operation. Shops tend to meander here and there, tucking inside nonshops (like the bookstore in the basement of the Old South Meeting House) or sidling up against half-defined office spaces. This may be why some "insiders" fret about the inauthentic cheek-by-jowl accessibility of the renovated Quincy Market boutiques, despite these shops' success in stimulating city and street life and drawing Boston's largest clutch of walkers. Others may be heard to sigh for the awkward passageways lost with the destruction of the old Jordan Marsh maze.

Boston still abounds in recessed buildings, however. Sometimes their basic architectural service, and even style, is simply to line the streets. "Background buildings," in the vernacular of a few years ago, these old-timers of masonry—granite, sandstone, brick—hew to the courteous limits of downtown Boston's former 125-foot ceiling. They follow the same orderly plane along the sidewalk and supply window space evenhandedly to a pristine white Fanny Farmer's or a woodsy emporium for platform clogs and jeans. True, the 1960s' invasion of architectural egos gave us megalithic intruders (if also some prize-winning designs). Too many highrises that turn their blank windows, wind corridors, and barren curtain walls to the passer-by can destroy pedestrian turf. For all the drama of Boston's waterfront revival, so much renewal seems a spider-plant conspiracy—hanging pots have replaced shredded curtains. One sometimes wonders whether all the spanking-new office buildings and recyclings come close to recouping the loss of one real, if seedy, neighborhood such as the West End.

Nonetheless, Boston has smothered less of the past than most cities; it has sacrificed less of its urban landscape to the Gods of Progress. Call it obstinate or enlightened, the city has a tradition of holding out against what the nineteenth century called "mere utility." Before the turn of the century, Bostonians had voted to bury the trolley in America's first municipal subway, ridding the town of an early multiwheel monster. Though streetcars were the "gondolas of the people" and the path to urban advancement, the city's progressive citizens—from the future Supreme Court Justice Louis Brandeis to merchant prince Edward Filene and former mayor Frederick O. Prince—fought the "Battle of the El" against developer Henry Whitney: rather than despoil the Common or mar Tremont Street with the noise and grime of an elevated, the city pioneered in tunneling underground. Boston also won the country's first height limitations on buildings, initially for itself—125 feet downtown, 70 feet near the border of parks, and 90 feet at Copley Square—then for other cities, with a Supreme Court decision in 1903. Such adjectives as *restrained* and *limited*, key words for a truly pedestrian city, ruled here, first as fiat, then as attitude. They will surface, urbanists hope, to down the leisure-suited high-risers and greedy realtors who would lay waste to the walker's city.

Such modesty and reticence could be catching; they should certainly be encouraged. I have often thought that a prize in *civility* (stemming from the same root as *city*, after all) would reflect more glory upon the Boston Society of Architects than their Harleston Parker Medal for *excellence* (*excel* means "surpass"). Another simple step—one that, I admit, appeals especially to a writer—would be the creation of a new kind of licenser: a licenser of addresses. Such a person, or board, would authorize the street address or name of every new building. By this easy means the city could outlaw all such singular blockbuster names as "The Prudential," rejecting out of hand the nomenclature of the Merchants, the Shawmut, and the First National Bank buildings, and refusing the exalted street numbers "One" and "100," as in *One* Boston Place, *One* Beacon Street, *One* Center Plaza, and *100* Federal Street. These self-inflating labels symbolize the arrogant architecture of the last decade, designs quite alien to the humane streets and style that define the walking city. "Something went wrong," as Edward Logue, head of the Boston Redevelopment Authority in the boom years, confessed to a design conference. "We moved from a higher to a lower standard." Could arrogant, unneighborly structures rise under such unexceptional digits as 13 Federal or 89 Devonshire Street? I doubt it. Where is the status in such names? Better still, consider a scheme of half digits—recall that the Boston Athenaeum, a magnificent library if there ever was one, bears the modest number 10½ Beacon Street.

I was never so convinced of the foot-bound nature of Boston's architecture as the year when back troubles deprived me of some of my own foot power. In the midst of writing an urban-design history, *Lost Boston*, I moved through the city in a horizontal posture, lying in the backseat of car or cab, casting my eyes on the tops of buildings. During the ordeal I liked to fancy all the benefits of my new point of view—the cornices carefully considered, the turrets studied, the polychrome panels dissected, the appreciation of the details with which Boston's architects adorned their buildings. One day from my almost upside-down perch I even saw the mayor, utterly alone atop a balcony overlooking the Common and Beacon Street, inhaling the day and the city with a joy that convinced me, despite my momentary pique at his political actions, that he too took pleasure in the beauty of his town. How I relished the gnarled wall-climbing wisteria in the springtime, the snow patterned on handsome copper roofs in winter. Between my research and this enforced outlook, I gained a new perspective—never had I learned more about Boston's architecture, I declared to all. In fact, I congratulated myself much too loud and much too long. Never had I felt more estranged from the city that I described. The car's pace was too fast, the distances covered were too great, the time and space sequence was out of whack. I had lost Boston, the walking city.

This is not to say that a pedestrian city must be a city fixed for all time by the first builders, to remain static ever after. The structure and open spaces of a walking city, of any living city, must change to a degree or die. But how and how much they change are critical. The best change in Boston has come in nineteenth-century rhythms, and although these rhythms were not supersonic, they had fine momentum and enormous power to alter for the good. Growing toward the end of its fourth century, Boston again must set the pace. Will it be the sightless speed of the freeway or the seeing step of the pedestrian? For almost 350 years the city has limned a pattern sympathetic to the amble of the walker. I hope it will endure. For, whether the walker is a ragtag eccentric or groomed to an inch of our "Edward Everetts," this pattern remains the yardstick for the city's humane architecture of all time and times to come.

"East View of Faneuil Hall Market," drawn on stone by J. Andrews, *lithograph by Pendleton, 1827.* BOSTON ATHENAEUM

OPPOSITE: *Quincy Market, 1977. Photograph by Steve Rosenthal.*
BENJAMIN THOMPSON & ASSOCIATES, INC., ARCHITECTS

Academic Asset

Boston's student population is the densest in the nation—
    Wall to wall and halfway up the ivory tower.
It's a vast accumulation of such massive concentration
    That it lights the town by Ph.Diesel power.

With such hordes of scholars churning up the cream of higher learning
    In a hotly burning passion for their goals,
Little wonder there are plenty of the local cognoscenti
    Who have joined the group for whom the Nobel tolls.

Though the Commonwealth's assessors have neglected its professors
    (Since their salaries don't garner much respect),
Still the State might find a cheering source of revenue appearing
    If it ever tried to tax the intellect.

Boston Latin School, 1892. Photograph by A. H. Folsom. BOSTON PUBLIC LIBRARY

Daguerreotype showing the children of Nathan and Harriet Appleton:
Hattie, Willie and Natey with their dog Bruno, 1851. SOCIETY FOR THE
PRESERVATION OF NEW ENGLAND ANTIQUITIES

"Who Needs No Introduction . . ."

Since I married and left Boston in 1928, it might be imagined that I would have nothing to say about my birthplace. On the contrary. I love Boston, and I have been learning over most of a lifetime how to observe one of the most interesting things about interesting Boston: its relations vis-à-vis the outside world. Long before the day when John Murray Forbes, aged seventeen, sailed up the Yangtze River in November of 1830 and was met at its head by the merchant Hu Kwa (worth $26,000,000)—whose mainstay Forbes promptly and lucratively became—Boston had been meeting the world in its own special way, and was being met by it with surprising consistency. For if Southerners are loved and New Yorkers are envied (or used to be), Bostonians, generally, are met with respect.

The great thing about Boston in the outside world is that almost everyone knows what Boston is, or thinks he does. Not necessarily *where* it is (an English writer said to me, "Born in Boston? You must know my cousin Cecily. She's married to our consul in Viña."). *What* Boston is, to the world outside, is a name: a name for something very definite. The same cannot quite be said of any other American city.

When my great-uncle Charles Hale was being measured for his official uniform as consul general to Egypt (diplomatic uniforms were subsequently banned by a resolution in Congress in 1867), the tailor remarked that his grandfather had made the uniform worn by John Adams, first American minister to the court of St. James's; his father had made John Quincy Adams's; and he himself had made that of the present incumbent, Charles Francis Adams. "Proper sort of city, Boston, if I may say so, sir" is how the tailor is supposed to have topped it off. Did he, perhaps, coin the phrase made familiar by *The Proper Bostonians*? (In Amory's book, I should add, my family, never having made or, like the Adamses, acquired any money, is termed merely "illustrious." But I am talking about just Boston.)

Charles Hale's sister Susan, on her way to visit him in Cairo, breakfasted at Shepheard's Hotel on her customary soft-boiled eggs, which she broke over a piece of toast. An English lady at the next table viewed her closely, meanwhile, and was moved to say, "That must be very nasty."

"I shouldn't be eating it if it were," replied Aunt Susan. She pronounced it "ware."

"Boston lady, I presume?" said her interlocutor. Or so the story ends.

Out in the world Bostonians do tend to come on a bit strong. The current Charles Francis Adams, longtime chief executive of the Raytheon Company, is reported to have sailed in Buzzards Bay on a collision course with a freighter. Adams's fifty-foot cutter, *Auk III*, itself of old Boston lineage, forced the big ship to a complete stop, screws screaming in reverse. The freighter's skipper, standing on his bridge in a foaming rage, shouted down, "Who are you, and what right have you to pull this goddamned stunt?" "The name is Charles Francis Adams," the answer floated across the waters, "and I have the right of way."

In my younger days, out in the world, I managed to come on a bit strong myself, without meaning to. I used to dine at the house of the hospitable James Southall Wilson—English-department chairman and dean of the faculty at the University of Virginia—a Virginian and married to a granddaughter of President Tyler. I remember with horror asking one day at table, dreamily but sincerely seeking information, "Why do boys go to little colleges like the University of Virginia when there *is* Harvard?" *I* had not so much as gone to Radcliffe, but by thinking of the boys' families as Bostonians I tended to anticipate family therapy. Dear man, he did not retort. He was fond of me, but he did rather get even, for he used to say, not occasionally but every time I saw him, "You can always tell a Harvard man, but you can't tell a Harvard man much . . ."

My gaffe, completely without intention, reveals another, mysterious facet of "coming from Boston." When I left, at twenty, in full rebellion against what really were Boston's assorted rigidities, I was under the impression that I was anything but Bostonian. But if you are from Boston, Bostonianism is expected of you. The Winsor School had taught me the Civil War for a month or two, in American-history year, but when in the thirties I reached Virginia, Civil War battles were still being fought hot and heavy over dinner tables.

"What did your grandfather do in the War Between the States?" asked the young hothead lawyer. "He was a clergyman in Boston," I said. "Then your grandfather was a coward," he replied.

I began to find the most extraordinary opinions coming out in me, which I hadn't known I possessed. Inherited opinions, I would say, except that the policy of the *Boston Daily Advertiser*, which my family then ran (and mostly wrote), was before the outbreak of that war's hostilities conciliatory, and afterwards, though firmly Unionist, moderate. What I heard coming out of my mouth were more Garrisonian sentiments. (A member of the Garrison family did get named after a member of mine, but there was no intermarrying, so I could not have inherited their opinions. I must have inhaled them.)

I hasten to add that things have, since 1954, cooled off considerably down in this other American commonwealth, and that I have, by much the same dynamic as with Boston, become to some happy degree Virginian. (This must be immediately evident, because earlier I should never have been uninhibited enough to write of my forebears.) I still get called a Yankee in the South, and it is not meant as a compliment. But, whereas to Europeans a Yankee means any American, and to Southerners a Yankee means any Northerner, and to Northerners a Yankee means any New Englander, to New Englanders a Yankee means a farmer of old English stock from Maine, New Hampshire, or Vermont; as such, a Yankee is an absolute pearl without price. So how could I mind? Little by little, as life's choices have had to be made and decisions taken, I have recognized what, actually, I was all the time. Some are born Bostonians, some few acquire Bostonianism, and some have Bostonianism come out in them.

It is still more mysterious, when one is hatching out one's Bostonianism, to realize what things the world takes Boston to be. People are quite clear and definite in their minds about Boston, and often attempt to prove their views factual. But there is no getting around it: the world's view is that of a Puritan stereotype, and as such, wildly inaccurate, a fantasy founded on the past. In this view Boston is of course shockable—was it not the home of the Watch and Ward Society? Boston is inhospitable, continues the legend. Boston is cold, Boston is unattractively highbrow, Boston hangs on to its money to a degree that would be absurd if it were not so avaricious. Boston is snobbish, thinking no spot so high as Beacon Hill.

Sometimes, surrounded with miscellaneous misinformation, one begins to fear one has become prim, inhospitable, chilly, a bluestocking, and penurious, as if to satisfy the world's demand. But Beacon Hill? Beacon Hill, indeed! What about Boston's social upheavals since I left in 1928? *Beacon Hill!* How about the high-technology factories, the electronics laboratories that line Route 128? How about developments like the Prudential Center, sprung— and not recently, either—from one of the dreariest parts of the Back Bay? The ramps and parkways that render Boston as unlike its Victorian image as the landscape of the moon? There is no living in the past with that; everything is change and renewal.

But you do not love someone for his technological know-how, but rather for his quality of truly being what he ineffably is. There is something *to* those stereotypical puritanisms—they were, indeed, just what I was rebelling against. Older friends in Boston, even today, do add in a whisper, "And we'll have a *drink!*" I myself hate to have even best-loved friends drop in; I have things I want to do. It irritates my friends that I insist a television set would get in the way of my reading as much as I want to read. It does horrify me (unrealistically, I am told) when my Virginia lawyer suggests I go into principal. As for Boston's far-famed snobbery, I am a terrible snob— about words and the English language.

Another element shines like a star through the murk of the stereotype. There seems to be, perhaps there always has been, a national, even international respect for the virtues of Boston's very defects. In a world torn by suicidal conflicts and creeping despair, Boston seems to stand for something less unstable, more consistent, possibly, after all, wiser. The respect is sometimes reluctant—but then, it always must be.

Of Dr. William Everett, son of Edward Everett and a professor of classics, Samuel Eliot Morison told a tale that illustrates this quality. Everett was "unattractively highbrow," if you will, and he carried untidiness to a point where he was nicknamed Piggy.* While Everett's father was minister to the Court of St. James's, Will had gone to Trinity College, Cambridge, where one of his college friends was the Prince of Wales. Fifty years later, when our ambassador to England was a former student of Will's, the Honorable Joseph Choate, old Will decided, on a trip to England, that he would like to look up his old friend, now King Edward VII. Presenting himself at the American embassy on Grosvenor Street, he asked that a note be sent around to Buckingham Palace. The clerks, taking him for some particularly shabby old eccentric, demurred; Will Everett then demanded that they send his card up to the ambassador.

Moments later Joe Choate came bounding down the stairs, hands outstretched, and ordered the staff to do whatever his dear old friend Dr. Everett might ask. The note was sent around to Buckingham Palace, the clerks winking and quietly sniggering as Will waited. In half an hour a royal brougham drew up at the door, and a footman brought in a note, which Will proceeded to read aloud to the staff. Its burden was: "Dear Everett, You have neglected me shamefully all these years. Come at once to the Palace and we will talk about old days. Faithfully yours, Edward R et I." And without more ado, away drove messy old Will to call on the King.

Today I feel a quiet pride in Boston. Like my old school there, it seems to grow better and younger all the time. When my second son graduated from Harvard I came home from Oxford, where my husband had been giving the Lyell Lectures, to watch his commencement. I remember wondering how the old Yard would hold up, after the glorious quads of Magdelen, New College, and Merton. Not to worry. The Yard looked fine. There was no more

---

* Everett's cousins the Hales were called The Dirty Delightfuls; Morison's grandfather, standing at his Brimmer Street window, exclaimed, "There goes Ned Hale. Can't he ever learn that a gentleman always wears gloves?" And indeed, Edward Everett Hale sometimes wore evening clothes all day long to avoid having to change.

glorious sight than the academic procession, headed by the sheriffs of Middlesex and Suffolk counties. In it, professors who in ordinary life might be miserly, dull, unappreciative, unkind, seemed transfigured; for they had all worked, they had done what they must do to wear those hoods, they had labored, they were learned. I seemed to see them for what they meant. They were devoted, serious, and noble. They were Harvard.

Just so Boston. Despite its very real failures, despite its severe racial and ethnic tensions, Boston persists in conferring a sort of talismanic value that (as a doctor in San Francisco, son of a Czech immigrant, wrote me) gives people a sense of security. On its 350th anniversary, it is a sort of benefaction Boston makes to the world.

From my vantage point outside, I can see how Boston represents a quintessential part of the nation's psyche. A reader of mine in Santa Fe, who had been one of the 1969 dissidents at Harvard, writes that there is something reassuring to her, that Boston can at the same time be both haven for the flower children and one of America's most conservative strongholds. Is the paradox partly responsible for Boston's continuing power to renew itself—whose outward and visible signs are in such phenomena as Government Center, with its accompanying Quincy and Faneuil Hall Markets?

Whether grudgingly or affectionately or resignedly, the country appears to find that Boston epitomizes its conscience, its intellectual fortitude, its financial prudence, its dignity, its ability once in a while to (as a transplanted Bostonian in New York put it) keep its trap shut. Boston, taken in this splendid sense, turns once more of course into sheer myth, mere stereotype. But an eternal quality of myth is that it is indispensable, too, and profoundly real and true.

OPPOSITE: *Edward Everett Hale at Matunuck, Rhode Island, ca. 1905.* THE BOSTONIAN SOCIETY

Mayor James Michael Curley with school children at the Benjamin Franklin monument, Old City Hall, School Street. BOSTON ATHENAEUM

ALAN LUPO

This Is What Politics Is

A View from the Cosmos:

"Massachusetts has been the wheel within New England, and Boston, the wheel within Massachusetts. Boston, therefore, is often called the 'hub of the world,' since it has been the source and fountain of the ideas that have reared and made America." —The Reverend F. B. Zinckle, 1868.

A View from the Ward Rooms:

"No land was ever saved by little clubs of female faddists, old gentlemen with disordered livers or pessimists cackling over imaginary good old days, ignoring the sunlit present. What we need in this part of the country are men and mothers of men, not gabbing spinsters and dog-raising matrons in federation assembled." —James Michael Curley, four times mayor of Boston.

A View from the Street:

"Let's cut the baloney and get rid of the phoney." —A subtle piece of modern media advertising in the form of a sign tacked onto a trailer truck parked opposite the target's headquarters, 1978.

The Democrats from the ward were meeting upstairs over a bar on one of those days when the bar was not having a fire or some other featured event. Meeting over a bar did not seem too wonderful an idea, given the mood and history of such gatherings.

After a few minutes of pleasantries and other noises, somebody announced that nobody else could come in and register for the official ward-committee meeting, which was supposed to be a George McGovern-type grass-roots-party meeting to determine who should go to Kansas City someday and discuss Great Issues.

The announcement unlocked the door to about forty years of Byzantine bickering, unsettled wars, family feuds, anger over jobs never delivered. It seemed there were at least two ward committees, one pledged to Mayor Kevin Hagan White, and the other to Joseph Timilty, who wished to be mayor.

"They were fighting over who should be the delegates to Mecca," one guy remembered. "It was the usual stuff. Qualifications of eligible voters. Who gets to set the rules. Why wasn't there more advertising? Both groups were trying to stack the meeting, and the first group that got there gaveled the second group out. The biggest guy in the room was with the mayor. You could say he played a very active role."

Given that confusion had taken hold of the meeting, the Boston Democrats reverted to tradition and began slugging one another. First they started slugging inside. Then the big guy would grab somebody by the neck and invite him to be slugged outside, so as not to bloody up the establishment.

A couple of guys with a vested interest in protecting the immediate neighborhood from sudden-death urban renewal went down to the station house, where the cop on duty agreed such a situation undoubtedly warranted the attention of law-enforcement authorities, but, it being Saturday, he had only one cruiser out, and the guys were on their lunch hour.

Meanwhile, across town, a whole bunch of relatively liberal Democrats who were taking this issues business seriously had started out their day in a sincere attempt to attend their local ward-committee meeting. They never found it. A local state representative who pretty much ran the ward committee, and wouldn't know a McGovern if he tripped over him, got his old pals together for five or ten minutes in a building very few persons seemed to be able to find, declared the meeting open, and, there being no further business, declared it closed.

Some Bostonians look upon such activities and suggest that politics is the city's number-one sport, for both participants and observers, greater even than the fabled Red Sox. They are correct, but they do not go far enough. Politics is also the city's biggest growth industry. It has outlasted the slave trade, the rum trade, the China trade, the fishing trade, the shoe trade, the garment trade, and a whole era of mass-produced literary masterpieces, also a trade.

It is our institutionalized sweatshop, nonunion, open to all willing to work long hours at no pay so that they may someday work even longer hours at adequate pay or, in certain cases, hardly any hours for outrageous pay in the industry's by-product production line, which people call government.

The industry is a family business. The first families said public service (which is politics) was a trust. In addition to its being a public trust, it was a family trust—Winthrops, Bradfords, Lodges, Cabots, Quincys, Saltonstalls. Other families quickly grasped the idea.

Senator Edward M. Kennedy is the grandson of two ward heelers, Patrick Kennedy, who ran a saloon in East Boston and who is now an elementary school, and John F. "Honey Fitz" Fitzgerald, who ran the North End, served twice as mayor, and is now an expressway.

Mayor Kevin Hagan White is the son of a state senator and city council president, the grandson of a city council president, and the son-in-law of a city council president.

State senator Joseph Timilty is the nephew of a police commissioner and mayoral candidate, and grandson of a state senator lovingly called "Diamond Jim" Timilty.

Former school committeeman David Finnegan, who, like Timilty, has wished to become mayor, is the brother of a state representative, and they are the sons of a state senator.

Former city councillor Louise Day Hicks, who used to run against White for mayor, is the daughter of a judge. City councillor Patrick McDonough is the brother of a school committeeman. City councillor Frederick Langone is the brother of a politician, and they are of the third generation of a political family. Lieutenant Governor Thomas O'Neill, of Boston, is the son of Speaker of the U.S. House "Tip" O'Neill, himself the son of a man who mastered the political intricacies of the sewer system of Cambridge, a city that, though not the main subject of this book, extends the influence of Boston.

One need not be an elected official to remain in his or her family's good graces. The public-employment lists are loaded with fathers, uncles, mothers, aunts, sisters, brothers, sons, daughters, and in-laws of those who have inherited the Yankee legacy.

As the older generation passes on, they become roads, schools, overpasses, and public washrooms. The progeny then take up the family business, but it is not a simple matter of inheritance. Unlike the private sector, in politics one must indeed run for the position. Very much like the private sector, one picks trusted friends and associates to help the running and subsequent governing.

Instead of filing papers of incorporation, those involved in Boston politics organize committees. Less polite observers call the committees machines. The organization is sometimes called a "friendship committee," which, if not subtle, is at least accurate.

"What are the election issues?" Boston visitors ask.

The issues are how many old high-school or football-team friends or cousins are still living in the district, and will they love you in September as they did years ago at Boston Latin or Dorchester High? Such persons are called workers. They are students of a very old math called precinct returns. They major in election results, computing the number of doors that must be knocked on, the number of apartments to be leafleted, the number of cars needed to carry voters from nursing homes to the polls. These people may have flunked high-school algebra. They may be losers when it comes to hitting the daily number. But they know precincts the way artists know colors.

These people are so good that every four years presidential candidates pluck them out of those precincts to do in other states what they do annually in Boston. The city's precincts, it seems, are the Triple A league for national elections. For the parochial, insular Bostonian, only two events have drawn him elsewhere for more than a few months—World War II and national elections.

One exception is the Boston-Harvard-Wall Street-Washington route, a road on which the Christian Herters and Henry Shattucks, the Robert Cutlers and Henry Cabot Lodges and Bundy family members keep bumping into one another. Such men were given "appointments," while back in the precincts lesser-known pols got "jobs." Somehow, appointments are more highly regarded than jobs. The former are seen as exercising a public trust, while the latter are seen as exercising mere ambition.

Most of the job holders don't care, for they see politics as a means to an end, which is defined as more politics, or making a living. They believe all politics are local. So, Tip O'Neill sits in Washington as Speaker of the House and tells young congressmen stories of how you can lose it all if you lose touch with the precincts and forget to knock on the doors of the faithful.

Boston's pols are often uncomfortable in Washington. Curley preferred City Hall to Congress, as does Louise Day Hicks. In the late 1800s Patrick A. Collins, who would become a congressman, a mayor, and then a statue on the Commonwealth Avenue mall, saw national politics for what it was—and is:

In practice, the congressman is an errand boy. He must secure places for the men who gave him their support, pensions for veteran soldiers and sailors, pardons for those who are in prison, and discharges for all young men who tire of their services after enlistment in the military and naval branches.... When any of his constituents or their sisters or their cousins or their aunts visit [sic] the capital, he must entertain them, take them to the theatre, show them over the Capitol and the White House and all its departments without murmur.

And when he is a candidate for reelection, if the district be close, he must pay heavily for the privilege of going to Washington for another term to do the same kind of drudgery over again.... If we continue in our present course, wealth will control all the avenues to honest political distinction....

The Boston precinct worker packs his parochial pride in his suitcase. If one should stumble upon him in a campaign headquarters in another city, he will grin and shake his head with disbelief and say with obnoxious pride—as one of Ted Kennedy's men said in Baltimore years ago—"What's wrong with these people down here? They don't even know how to run a rally. We had to dig up the drum-and-bugle corps!"

What one does with the public trust, when one gets it, is another story. There is a constant pulling and tugging upon the mayor by the banks and downtown corporate interests on one side, and by the neighborhoods—the essence of the city, its uniqueness and its insularity together—on the other.

Boston has a reputation for skulduggery and boondoggling in politics, but its politics are no worse than elsewhere and probably cleaner than most Southern county courthouses, the ward rooms of Chicago, and the capital of any state currently enjoying a real-estate growth spurt. Boston's problem is not corruption, but that its corruption is rarely subtle, which is to say that the problem in the city is less harmful than that of a suburb, where corruption is closer to the chest of the players and less likely to be examined by the heavy press and media.

"Politics and holiness are not always synonymous," James Michael Curley said. "There are times . . . when, if you wish to win an election, you must do unto others as they wish to do unto you, but you must do it first."

There marked the difference between the Curleys of Boston and their corporate critics. A Curley was simply saying what both he and a banker were prone to do. The banker, however, would not acknowledge such a crass observation, though it might be accurate. It all depends on one's definition of corruption. To the "reformers," the Establishment figures who met quietly in boardrooms far from the din of an election rally, corruption was fattening the public payroll and playing games with the tax rates. To the pols, corruption was the very economic system run by their critics, the Establishment, a system that failed to use its economic power for the benefit of those most in need.

Those who scolded the Boston Irish politicians for such philosophies as espoused by Curley were also neglecting their own history.

Hanging or otherwise eliminating Quakers was hardly subtle, but it was a political act by Puritans worried about an erosion of faith in the precincts.

King George's sporadic attempts to mollify the Yankee Sons of Liberty with a concession or two sent the town-meeting members packing into Faneuil Hall, where they acted pretty much like the boys upstairs over the bar in the ward-committee meeting. "Wherever there is a spark, we will kindle it," Samuel Adams counseled.

The spark was a beacon of sorts for generations to come. The message seemed to be that if life is short, political life is even shorter; given the time available, why not a frontal assault through the swinging doors?

Why not bring in out-of-towners, set them up overnight on election eve in a rooming house (mattress voters, they came to be called), and let them vote the next day. Let them vote often, for after all, election day was only once a year.

Why not plant one of your own men at a rally to scream that you were a bum, a discredit to your race, family, and religion, and then disappear, as you regaled the audience with charity toward your detractor and a laundry list of what you had done for those assembled?

Why not register the dead to vote? Should death automatically end an American's suffrage?

When reforms put an end to such activities, that meant only that a politician's imagination was to be challenged. In one recent election, a candidate reported having received a thousand dollars from a local political figure, a truly miraculous gift in this instance, given that the donor had died sometime earlier than the gift was allegedly given.

Barely anyone noticed, not that anything would have been done anyway. First, it was hard enough to enforce campaign-contribution regulations among the living, much less the departed. Second, if a man can't vote anymore after he has passed away, why can't he at least contribute to the campaigns of the living?

These are not the subtleties of advance men, media manipulators, and poll-takers or image makers. They are the sparks that kindle. They are the acts of the outrageous, the roar of Kitty Craven, a former city councillor who brought the uttering of obscenities from the gutter to an art form as she glared at a councillor and yelled, "You baldheaded bastard," before she pitched an ashtray at him.

They are the exuberances of the late Julie Ansel, who represented the now defunct Jewish wards, as he rushed to the airport to greet a sick constituent being brought home from Miami, ran up the gangway to help grab the stretcher, and managed to pitch the woman over the side.

They are the mixed metaphors of a councillor's answer to a school committeeman testifying that what this city needed was more "expertiseness": "Let's call a spade a spade. I never run around the mulberry bush. I always get to the meat of the problem."

Indeed, if Boston politics lacks for anything, it is "expertiseness" and subtlety.

Shortly after the turn of the century, when corruption was highly visible, there was organized the Boston Finance Commission (the FinCom, as it's still called today) to monitor the city's sins. In one report the commission noted that the superintendent of supplies, at the time of his appointment, was chairman of a Republican ward committee in East Boston, "and his selection seems to have been a political one." The FinCom proved more subtle in its conclusion than did the gentleman under question. He told the FinCom he generally ordered both Portland and common cement.

"What kind of Portland cement?"

"Regular Portland cement, furnished from the Portland manufacturing companies."

"Where are they located?"

"They are located down in Maine. Sometimes it is made out of the rock, and then there are cements that are made out of clamshells, you know."

He told the FinCom he had even written to the "manufacturers down in Maine, where they manufacture the goods."

The FinCom shook its collective head and noted, "The fact is that no Portland or other commercial cement is made in Maine, and there are no manufacturers of cement there to whom he could have written. When asked to produce copies of his letters, he was unable to do so."

A few weeks later, the man said he really had meant Pennsylvania, not Maine. No, he still couldn't find any letters.

About the same time, the FinCom wanted to know why there was such a dramatic increase in the collection and killing of stray doggies. The constable in charge was getting a buck a dog. Body counts were tried, but with no success. Could he produce records?

Well, he had kept a book, but somebody broke into his place, and, wouldn't you know, they stole the doggie book.

The corrupt were not subtle, but they were, in their own fashion, honest. The man in charge of Boston's coal supplies was subjected to FinCom interrogation:

"Did you know anything about coal?"

"Not a thing."

"Did you know how to test it?"

"No."

"Did you know whether a test could be made?"

"No."

"What difference would it make whether you bought Georges Creek coal, New River coal, or other coal?"

"I don't know."

"Did you ever see a bill of lading?"

"Never."

When the same FinCom, however, nitpicked about nickel-and-dime savings, the politicians wondered what in the name of reality one should be worried about—anal form filling or impoverished residents.

The Boston politician came to discern some hypocrisy, a double standard among certain reformers and good-government committees. If industries could gouge the laborer or throw him out of work, should not government or politics give him sustenance?

If the private sector asked for a man's money, and the churches for his soul, could not the politician ask him for his vote?

"Politics is not the dirty game that some of our holier-than-thou people would have the world believe," said Martin Lomasney, who ruled Boston's West End. "When it comes down to serving the people, the practical politician, whether you call him ward heeler, boss, or henchman, has it all over the genius, the statesman, and the great thinker. And this is simply because the practical politician knows mankind and human nature, knows the whims, the fancies, and the needs of the man in the street."

Whatever their faults, Lomasney, Curley, and others watched the private sector desert New England for faster bucks elsewhere, and perceived the hypocrisy.

The ward heelers and their successors have taken the Yankee stronghold of politics, but not the boardrooms of private power. The successors, mainly Irish, Italians (for a while, the Jews), and now, slowly, blacks and Hispanics, have blended pragmatic street politics of their times with that of Sam Adams.

But perhaps more important for history is yet another blending, a sense of statesmanship and public service that the very history and age of the city tend to inspire among many who serve in its public councils. It is not that Boston has somehow cornered the market on morality. It's just that Boston has been around for so long, when Beacon Hill was precisely that, because a beacon of fire was hoisted there as a signal for ships in the harbor.

The beacon of fire is long gone, but the spark that kindles remains, and, perhaps, it has become the beacon signaling a direction for issues that we still debate.

Shortly before he became the second mayor of the city, Josiah Quincy was speaking in 1822 of poverty and crime: "Poverty, vice and crime, in the degree in which they are witnessed in our day, are, in fact, in some measure the necessary consequences of the social state."

In a community that would rather have believed that such conditions were simply the handiwork of God, Quincy was charting a radical, but sensible and courageous new course.

Josiah Quincy was a Boston pol.

One century ago, when Boston celebrated its 250th anniversary with much oration and too much pomp, a city councilman named Andrew O'Dowd was arguing that the council should get involved in raising the pay of laborers:

"I don't imagine for a moment that any one in this Common Council will consider in connection with the high prices of all articles constituting the necessaries of life, that an increase of wages is an unreasonable thing to be granted to the laborers. The mere matter of a dollar and a half a day is a small thing for a laborer upon which to support his family and properly educate his children."

O'Dowd was a Boston pol.

A few years ago, as this city first struggled through the trauma of court-ordered busing, Mayor Kevin White pleaded with the varied constituencies and neighborhoods that are Boston, pleaded with the inheritors of that dichotomy of love and hate implanted here more than 350 years ago:

"It's a tough time to be a senior in high school. It's a trying time to be the mother of an elementary-school child in Boston. And it's not the greatest time to be mayor of this city, either. But, it is our time, and we must make the best of it."

He, too, is a Boston pol.

But the politics of Boston, the basic commodity of the industry, is neither corruption nor statesmanship. It is the delivery of services.

Two years after the city's 250th anniversary, celebrated in 1880, a twelve-year-old boy arrived in Boston from a small town near Naples, a town then called Basilicata. Joseph Langone did not get much schooling, but many years later, when he died, he left a personal library of fifteen hundred books. He was a state representative, one of the first Italian-Americans in Boston to serve in public office.

His son, Joe, Jr., became a state senator. He was less patient than his father. Once, when he felt Curley had kept him waiting too long for an appointment, he kicked in part of Curley's door. During the Depression Joe, Jr., made a lot of trips to the relief office to speed up services to his constituents.

In the 1970s, Fred Langone, grandson of the immigrant, told a writer: "I've adopted the same policy. Anyone who comes here, I help. 'You can always see Langone' is my motto. This is what politics is."

As Boston neared that celebration a century ago, the Irish and other immigrants were beginning to build bases of political power. As the city enters its 350th year, blacks and Hispanics are flexing political muscles and talking of delivering services in exchange for votes.

"This is what politics is."

Boston City Hall, ca. 1865. Photograph by Josiah Johnson Hawes. BOSTON ATHENAEUM

Granary burial ground, established in 1660 on Tremont Street. BOSTON PUBLIC LIBRARY

OPPOSITE: "David Wood Stone," detail from an 18th century headstone, 1979. OLIVIA PARKER

Detail of the Saint-Gaudens Memorial on the Boston Common, honoring black and white soldiers who served the Union cause together with Robert Gould Shaw, and died with him July 18, 1863 (from the book Lay This Laurel, Eakins Press, 1973). RICHARD BENSON

OPPOSITE: Statue of Mary Dyer by Sylvia Shaw, erected at the State House in 1959. LEE FRIEDLANDER

MARY DYER

QUAKER

WITNESS FOR RELIGIOUS FREEDOM

HANGED ON BOSTON COMMON 1660

"MY LIFE NOT AVAILETH ME
IN COMPARISON TO THE
LIBERTY OF THE TRUTH"

FELICIA LAMPORT

Means Test

Boston isn't famous for displays of wealth—
　　Those who have the stuff would rather die than show it.
They feel that spending money may destroy one's health
　　And when they die they quietly bestow it.

Here and there are pockets of descendants of the greats
Who make their living managing their relatives' estates.

But by and large the children of the Boston rich
　　Who've stepped into their fathers' shoes (and suits)
Engage in public service at a fever pitch
　　And support the higher-learning institutes.

It's the deeply felt conviction of this active group
That the man who's merely wealthy is an incomepoop.

"New Boston and Charles River Basin," prospectus for an embankment by Charles Davenport, ca. 1886. Lithograph by J. H. Bufford's Sons. BOSTON ATHENAEUM

Harvard Class Races on the Charles River, May 1886.
JACK REPETTI ANTIQUES

Cambridge 02138

Elizabeth Hardwick once described Boston and Cambridge as two ends of the same mustache. Perhaps she really did see the two cities as being equally bushy. For me, Hardwick's image seems less apt than the one representing Cambridge as the brain and Boston as the nervous system of a large, complicated body, a body passionately in love with the Puritan ethic, trying to maintain its equilibrium in a madly secular world.

It is striking that although Cambridge occupies the same geographical relationship to Boston as, say, Brookline, it is definitely not a suburb and Brookline definitely is. Cantabrigians with any self-esteem would never dream of referring to themselves as suburbanites. We live in our own city, our own world.

There are a good many people in Cambridge who claim they do not need Boston. These must be the folks who hate sports and never go to Fenway Park or the Boston Garden, who don't require State Street help (either financial or legal), who are afraid of heights (the Hancock Tower sways queasily in the wind), who think the Ritz Bar isn't funky enough, who never travel anywhere (note that you cannot conveniently enter or leave Cambridge by air, rail, or Greyhound without going first into Boston), and to whom the idea of a Freedom Trail makes as much sense as a Bondage Trail. Cambridge needs Boston, of course, but for those things that could loosely be called "services." When it comes to the life of the mind, Cambridge is the ultimate shrine.

This is chiefly Harvard's fault. Although intellectually as heavy as Harvard, M.I.T. has had astonishingly little influence on Cambridge. M.I.T. is like a powerful engine below decks that throbs and energizes but remains, for all intents and purposes, invisible. Harvard, on the other hand, is so assertive in so many ways that it is impossible to think of Cambridge—especially 02138—without this "beloved Goliath," as one of my neighbors characterized it. Like Chartres and its cathedral, Cambridge without Harvard would be just another dot on the map of the provincial countryside.

Henry Adams wrote that Harvard was a "negative force," because neither he nor any of his friends took it seriously. One hundred-odd years later, Harvard is taken so seriously that people are always trying to put it down in an attempt to hang on to their own identity. A New York woman recently admitted to me that she was terrified of the "Big H." I should also report that she left her husband when, subsequently, he took a job with this university.

George Homans, a direct descendant of all the right Adamses and a world-renowned sociologist, claims that the moment a person gets a Harvard faculty appointment he (or *she*, though Homans doesn't say it this way) is automatically hoisted into the "upper class." By which he means, I think, an acceptance in a circle as exclusive as that of Mme. Verdurin's in Proust and as fragile as the roster of top rock stars. For woe to those who fail to produce regularly and whose product is not Grade A. I think of cows who fail to give milk—an unfair metaphor perhaps, but not, when you consider it, outrageous. The scorn to which a nonproducer is eventually subjected is sufficient to make the victim leave town altogether—which he or she usually does. Accomplishment is the highest expression of life here. In one three-block area there lived in Cambridge not so very long ago one Nobel and two Pulitzer prize winners, three people whose faces had appeared on the cover of *Time*, a presidential adviser, several novelists, a world-class psychiatrist, and a celebrated cook. (This is not counting a number of full professors at Harvard who had won honors in their fields; or academic deans and administrators too numerous to count.)

Along with the assumption that you will continue to produce until they carry you off in a box, Cambridge operates on the assumption that you will be quiet as a corpse about your accomplishments. The almost phobic horror of any sort of publicity is part of the symptomatology of the Cambridge/Boston condition, spreading back and forth across that ambiguous artery, the

Charles River, like malaria. A Cambridge author took two months to decide it wouldn't destroy him to hire a publicity agent to help promote his book. (By the time he made his decision, the book was dead in the stores.) The day a local historian won a prestigious award the only person to call him was the tailor, telling him his suit was ready. To appear in *People* or in a *Boston Globe* gossip column—though you may have had no part in arranging the story—is a disgrace roughly comparable to being shoved into a police lineup.

Harvard encourages murderous competition. It also demands experimentation and innovation—of a cerebral and aesthetic kind. Le Corbusier planned and executed for Harvard his only building on the North American continent. Called the Carpenter Center, it is an exuberant mass of sweeping curves, glass, and concrete, which, despite the cramped site it occupies, delivers an impression of structural luxury. A block away stands Gund Hall, a brilliantly utilitarian building, designed specifically for Harvard designers. Architecture is just one of countless means by which Harvard takes care of its own.

But it should be said that Harvard has been far less protective or supportive of the interests of those citizens of Cambridge and Boston who are not on the university rolls. In one effort to improve its civic image, Harvard recently started testing its homegrown educational theories and practices at the city of Cambridge's so-called Pilot School (which, incidentally, is housed in Harvard's old A. Lawrence Lowell Lecture Hall on Kirkland Street). It has also sponsored some imaginative and attractive low-income housing to counter its reputation as a slum lord. (The old traits keep showing up, however, as witness the monstrous diesel generating plant it is currently putting up in the Mission Hill section of Boston—one of the most densely populated low-income neighborhoods of the city. The generating plant will lower electrical costs for Harvard Medical School and the numerous hospitals in the area. How this will benefit the quality of the air breathed by residents of Mission Hill is somewhat less clear.)

Harvard's reputation and momentum are so powerful that were its Office of Public Communication to close down permanently, the university would continue to make intellectual waves. Like the Republican Party, Harvard is supremely self-confident and backed by enormous wealth. Unlike the G.O.P., however, it turns on more people than it turns off—all but those individuals who reject (or cannot cope with) its establishment stance and underlying elitism.

Harvard's relations with Boston University, Tufts, Boston College, Brandeis, and other educational centers in the area are generally cordial; but only M.I.T. seems to command the full respect of Harvard—and even at that, only in certain departments. It has been suggested that "State Street's primary role is to keep Harvard pure." It seems to me that what this really means is that some of Harvard's greatest benefactors have generously supported other universities in the area out of a sense of duty, but only Harvard out of real devotion.

In addition to its scholars, Cambridge, thanks to Harvard, attracts all manner of groupies. The number of lectures, concerts, poetry readings, art exhibits, movies, plays, and other improving events open to the Harvard community at any one time is staggering. Harvard even maintains an "arts hotline." On one spring day in 1978 it took a recorded voice four minutes and seventeen seconds to complete its telephonic spiel about events scheduled for one weekend. On a Saturday morning, whatever the weather, Harvard Square is as densely packed as Fenway Park during the World Series or Quincy Market at lunchtime. People come here to shop for things they can't find in Tewksbury or Dubuque, to share the torpor of the perennial students, and to receive an infusion of atmosphere laden with psychic and physical freedom, along with drifting hamburger grease.

Not all of Cambridge is Harvard. We should be grateful for that. North and East Cambridge and Cambridgeport do very well on their own, and make headlines only when local politicians like the redoubtable Al Vellucci demand that Harvard secede from the city—or, with prophetic seriousness, call for a moratorium on recombinant-DNA research. Mainly working-class, with substantial populations of first- and second-generation Americans, these Cambridge neighborhoods hold Harvard at arm's length, but hardly in awe.

And then there is Brattle Street, an anachronistic stretch of large houses on large plots of heavily taxed land tended by gardeners, protected by alarm systems, and shaded by elm, maple, linden, locust. Relatively few Harvard professors live in these mansions—not even Harvard pays that kind of salary—but Brattle Street sons and daughters (like their parents before them) almost invariably head for the Crimson diploma. It is from the Brattle Street area that dozens of State Street regulars walk to the Harvard Square subway entrance each morning and make the incredible seven-minute ride to the world of the stock and the brief. To these men (and women) Cambridge is a de facto suburb, whether they (or I) care to admit it. But do they live here simply because they prefer wood to brick?

My guess is that the mental voltage, and informality, fed as much by parsimony as by principle, keep them on this side of the river. Anyone who voluntarily boards the Red Line at Harvard Square *has* to be desperately in love with what makes Cambridge Cambridge.

For the subway station under the famous kiosk is squalor unparalleled: stygian, malodorous, and peeling all over, with a ceiling that rattles ominously when trains enter and depart. It seems appropriate that facing you, as you wait, is a poster extolling the services of a funeral parlor. The fact that this station in its present form will soon cease functioning is irrelevant—it's been in this moribund condition for a quarter of a century.

It is primarily the Yankee temperament that pervades Cambridge, having landed in Boston first and taken to its frigid climate. This temperament manifests itself in an absolute refusal to be with it in any respect except the intellectual. Thus, disco outfits and hot tubs will no doubt bypass Cambridge and all but a very small—and very young—segment of Boston. Styles change here with maddening slowness; the time lag for what is "in" seems to be roughly two decades. Twenty years ago when we moved from New York to Cambridge, my main sorrow was in leaving Bloomingdale's. Twenty years later Bloomingdale's arrived—albeit in Chestnut Hill—thrusting the Boston area at last into the twentieth century. Sister to this cultural quirk is the imperative to hide your riches—if you have any. The rich either spend their money "invisibly"—on investments or a new furnace—or they put it into real estate somewhere else. Money, in Cambridge, is at once disguised and disguising. Those who have it choose not to express their individuality through it. No turreted castles here, no borzois or game rooms.

Why do people leave New York for Cambridge, as I did? For us—my husband and two small children and I—the practical reasons were pedestrian and would have been true for any place with a decent library and a minimum of open space; we did not, in fact, have much choice. The other reasons have to do with a mind-set that rewards work for its intrinsic value rather than its noise, that keeps you honest by discouraging self-promotion, rates privacy above conformity, and allows you the freedom to be as informal as your own children.

Besides, where else can you find a cemetery through which the neighboring school takes its children on birdwalks, is ideal for cross-country skiing, and holds the remains of Mary Baker Eddy with a telephone beside her coffin, in case she feels like calling down to this heaven from that one?

The First Church of Christ, Scientist, 1911. Photograph by Baldwin Coolidge. SOCIETY FOR THE PRESERVATION OF NEW ENGLAND ANTIQUITIES

JUSTIN KAPLAN

The Party of the Present

A little over a century ago, literary Boston turned out in force to greet a fading prodigy from the Far West, Bret Harte, author of "The Luck of Roaring Camp" and "The Outcasts of Poker Flat." He dined at the Saturday Club with Longfellow, Lowell, Holmes, Emerson, Dana, and other great men who bore triple-barreled names uttered reverently in Jovian trochees and dactyls. After a few days of such company, Harte observed to his host, William Dean Howells, that in this part of the country it was impossible to fire off a revolver without bringing down the author of a two-volume work.

Howells chose to ignore the subintentional hostility of this quip. Literature in Boston, as he was to recall, "was so respectable, and often of so high a lineage, that to be a poet was not only to be good society, but almost to be good family." But it was clear even to Howells, who had come from Ohio as a literary pilgrim and postulant, that Boston culture had entered a post-Augustan age. He heard Dr. Holmes, who had few doubts about anything, tease a passing stranger with the advice "If you don't know where Washington Street is, you don't know anything." The guardians of Boston culture, it seemed, had ignored the warning Emerson had issued in his "Historic Notes of Life and Letters in New England": "There are always two parties, the party of the Past and the party of the Future; the Establishment and the Movement." The seedtime of Puritanism and the Revolution had produced a brilliant literary renaissance, but the harvest overripened. By the 1870s New England's great men had become its sacred cows. Mark Twain learned this when, on the occasion of Whittier's seventieth birthday, he gave what he believed was a humorous speech in which Emerson, Holmes, and Longfellow figured as tramps and cardsharps. Judging from the outcry, he might just as well have appeared in public without his pants on.

"The gentleman we have just been burying was a sweet and beautiful soul," the senile Emerson said in 1882 as he was leaving his friend Longfellow's funeral, "but I forget his name." He died a month later. His call for a breed of writers possessing nerve and dagger had apparently been forgotten, for there were few signs of a generation of worthy successors to take his place. As H. G. Wells said after the turn of the century, the mind of Boston simply had "filled up," like the Back Bay, and decided there was nothing more to be learned. High-caste Yankees occupied themselves with fitful reform movements and a cultural life that was merely Hubbish. During the 1880s *Leaves of Grass* was expelled from Boston and *Huckleberry Finn* was ostracized. The Watch and Ward Society, sponsored by men of impeccably "good society" and "good family," had begun the long sanitary sweep that in 1927 alone—a "banner year," according to Cleveland Amory— succeeded in removing from the bookstores works by Sinclair Lewis, Ernest Hemingway, John Dos Passos, Sherwood Anderson, Wells, and more than sixty other writers. If Boston was still the American Athens, it was the Athens not of Pericles but of the Thirty Tyrants. The ice age began to break up around the time of World War II. The title of Jean Stafford's novel *Boston Adventure* (1944) was suggestive of the change; so was the work of the Poets' Theater. The city's totemic figure, the late George Apley, was supplanted by the ebullient Skeffington of Edwin O'Connor's *The Last Hurrah*, a valedictory, like Marquand's novel, but also a salute to the spirit of pluralism and *aggiornamento* that was to bring a Boston Catholic to the White House.

Emerson's party of the future began to reassert itself and draw a steadily increasing number of writers to Boston. This time around, however, they have no desire to inhabit a self-sufficient literary capital. They know that New York has no rival now as a marketplace. Its book and magazine publishers occupy gleaming office towers. A scrambling subculture of agents, middlemen, publicists, and media contacts offer Vergil services on the path to literary success. Even Boston publishers fly down in the morning and back at night. But New York, as Walt Whitman once said, although a great place for writers to sell their produce, may not be the best place for them to grow it. Boston, with its cautionary history for writers, is now considerably more than an alternative city. It offers an alternative style.

Writers practice a notoriously independent, solitary, and even curmudgeonly profession that deals with the resistant material of language. Some Boston writers derive a moral satisfaction from being bound to their work by a hard winter, which closes down with such apparent finality that spring takes them by surprise. Perhaps, too, they are drawn here by a humane, patient tempo that nurtures memory and retrospection. Edward Everett Hale, who lived until 1909, remembered the circles left on the grass in Boston Common by the tents of Lord Percy's encampment during the winter of 1775–1776. And as for scale, Boston's amiable skyline has been violated time and again, but the city can still be walked comfortably; the imagination feels at home here; and one has a sense of proprietary familiarity with streets and buildings and the train that crosses the Charles.

In contrast to the old order of things, most Boston writers today are geographical outsiders by birth and were drawn here in part by a vitality that was synonymous with New England at the start. "Our town is now threescore and eight years old," Cotton Mather said in 1698, but it was already "the metropolis of the whole English America. . . . O Boston!" Despite the damage done to its tax rolls as a consequence, Boston remains the nation's capital of higher education, and ever since American universities began offering employment, shelter, and intellectual nurture to professional writers, the city has attracted more than its share of them. Through some miracle of transmission, and against all odds in a mass culture, literary vitality and the instinct of workmanship survive in Boston in ways relatively unaffected by the competitive chatter and narcissistic displays of the great marketplace less than an hour away by air. This may be one of the few communities left in America where you can work away on a book for years without having your neighbors tap their foreheads after you pass them in the street. Most of them are simply respecting your privacy, but more than a few are themselves poets, novelists, biographers, journalists, historians of one sort or another, or general thinkers.

Recently, a constitutive meeting of the New England branch of P.E.N., the international writer's guild, addressed itself to the topic "Why I Live 'Here' and Not 'There,'" "There," of course, meaning the other place. Robert Manning, a native of Binghamton, New York, and the editor of *The Atlantic Monthly*—the venerable journal to which Dr. Holmes stood godfather—said that Boston was an ideal place for writers and editors to find out what goes on in America at large. The writers who were meeting for the first time as a group—at the Boston Athenaeum, a monument to the old order—were surprised to realize how many others were there in the same room and how little contact they had been accustomed to having with one another. Some, such as the novelist John Updike, seemed mildly fearful that even a loosely knit professional organization of Boston writers might threaten the whole purpose of living here and not There, the freedom to escape the literary life, if one chooses, or at least to live in quiet little pockets or cells with other writers. The range of views and of levels of contentment was considerable, but nearly everyone seemed to be remembering, if only subliminally, a time when Boston writers got themselves too well organized.

OPPOSITE: *Daguerreotype of Dr. Oliver Wendell Holmes at age forty, 1849.* SOCIETY FOR THE PRESERVATION OF NEW ENGLAND ANTIQUITIES

H. H. Hunnewell and Professor C. S. Sargent at the opening exhibition of Horticultural Hall, 1901. BOSTON PUBLIC LIBRARY

One in the Sun, Joe

During the summer of 1968, about once a week, I would take the subway from the world in Cambridge to that other world in Boston. I would get off at the Arlington stop, proofread my manuscript while I walked, and arrive around noon at 8 Arlington Street, the offices of the Atlantic Monthly Company. There I would stand self-consciously in the lobby while a very proper-speaking receptionist called upstairs to confirm my luncheon appointment. Usually I would be very tired and nervous, having been at my typewriter all night; but the man who came down in the elevator would, through his presence, make me know that I was capable of much more than I believed. He was then seventy years old, but buoyant, effervescent. His handshake was firm, his eyes clear and direct. He was habitually cheerful. Tall, with that ramrod-stiff posture one associates with the British, he was absolutely neat in a tailored summer suit, starched shirt, and handcrafted tie. His dress, during that radical, masquerading summer, was sufficient to identify him with the forces of conservatism. Yet his smile and friendliness, the snappiness in his walk, suggested an energy, and perhaps a sense of purpose, far surpassing any I had encountered anywhere before. He was a hard man to keep up with.

We walked up Arlington Street toward the Ritz. Less than an hour before, usually, I would have been carrying out garbage in Cambridge; now, in Boston, showered but bearded, respectably dressed but still self-conscious, I moved with him through the crowds of stylishly dressed people going to the Public Garden. To the doorman at the Ritz we must have seemed an unusual pair. Yet my host was clearly on the best of terms with everyone there.

In the lobby he stood at the top of the steps leading down into the dining room, and when the maitre d', in his tuxedo, turned in our direction, my host lifted his arm casually and said in perfect, British-sounding English, in a voice that was self-assured and cheerful, "Two in the sun, Joe."

That summer Edward Weeks invited me to participate in a gentleman's ritual, many generations old. I did not know him well then, but I could hear in his voice an authority and ambience that were worlds away from my small world. This was, after all, the summer of 1968. Across the Charles River, in Cambridge, the antiwar movement was just beginning to gather momentum. Only three years before, as a college student in Atlanta, I might have been content to work as a waiter at the Ritz. Yet, through some strange and magical and undefined process, events had thrown together a graduate of a segregated Negro college and a man who seemed to be a Boston Brahmin. Moreover, this unlikeliest of associations was being put on display at the very elegant Ritz-Carlton. Whatever that magical process was, Edward Weeks seemed quite comfortable with it. I had crossed the dividing line between the excluded and the exclusive, and he had helped to make the process painless.

But from habit I watched the waiters and their movements. Also from habit, he looked casually around the room. "There's Kevin White," he said, nodding toward a dapper, gray-haired man at a table against the wall. "And next to him is Tom Winship, of The Boston Globe." An elderly woman being seated near our table called, "Hi, Ted." "Why, hello," he called back. "Lovely day, isn't it?" He chatted with the woman, introduced me to her. Then he said to me, "That's Avis De Voto. Her husband, Bernard, was a contributor of mine. He was an authority on Mark Twain." He spoke fondly of Bernard De Voto and recalled De Voto's account of the Boston dinner party, given in 1877 in honor of John Greenleaf Whittier, at which Mark Twain told a story that considerably embarrassed his hosts (Henry Houghton, Longfellow, Howells, and Holmes) and all of Boston literary society [see Justin Kaplan's "The Party of the Present," page 71—ed.] Edward Weeks laughed at the story, but took Mark Twain's side on the matter. He seemed to have an understanding of both Boston literary society and Mark Twain, and judged that Twain had been *fair* in his satire. For there was extraordinary candor in Edward Weeks, a profound sense of fairness, and it took me many years to realize that, more than most men in the country, he had helped to cause many of the good things that were then taking place outside the Ritz, in Cambridge, in the country, and in the rest of the world.

II

The one certain thing during those uncertain years was Edward Weeks's voice. It was the same fine instrument on paper that it was in conversation. Its precision and authority were what captivated initially; but what held one's attention, long after the tone of the voice was accepted, was the way he employed the instrument. Once you got comfortable with the tone, you began listening to what the words were *really* saying. They conveyed stories, very rich stories, pulled like fish from a flow of experience as rich and diverse and changing as this century has been. He spoke lovingly of people who were long dead—the great, the near great, and the obscure. He could look back in his memory to the earliest years of this century, to that last long moment of calm, and then move forward in time, commenting economically on the major events, the cheerful times, the changes. He defined the twentieth century not in terms of events but through people he himself had known, and the way in which events had touched them. He might begin with a name, pause briefly to reconstruct from memory what that person had actually said to him, pause again to recall his own reply, and then connect the exchange with some event that was historically significant.

I listened to him and learned. In recent years I have begun to understand that he was, and is, on intimate terms with a level of American society that, after Edith Wharton and J. P. Marquand and James Gould Cozzens, has been depicted only in the novels of Louis Auchincloss. American readers, and especially the broader American public, do not know about such people, who are called "upper-class" but remain as ill-defined as the people called "underclass." Many of them make great contributions while shunning publicity. They accept public duties privately, and perform them with no expectation of acclaim. Such people are rare, and are becoming rarer. They survive in personal memory rather than on the public record. They live on, after their deaths, only in the stories of their close friends; and because their friends usually share the same level of society, the stories have limited circulation. Unless a biographer is energetic enough, or insistent enough, to pursue them through the recollections of their friends, they are lost to history. The absence of their stories, and the values they dramatize, causes something vital to die out of our collective memory. In this special sense, the few people with such memories are repositories of a very rich tradition, and an opportunity to talk with them is a good occasion for the survival of some of their stories. Edward Weeks knew a lot of such people, and because he knew them he knows this century.

III

Through one of those accidents that are uniquely American, I came to meet Edward Weeks and learn a little about his tradition. Now, almost twelve years later, I am still learning. Through him I know a little bit extra about Ernest Hemingway, Walter Lippmann, Dr. Harvey Cushing, Bernard De Voto, Frederick Lewis Allen, Harold Ross, Joseph Henry Jackson, Mark De Wolfe Howe, and many other people who wrote books, did things, made lasting contributions. I have learned things that have helped me to appreciate the human dimensions of these people. I know that Catherine Drinker Bowen was dying of cancer when she was writing *The Most Dangerous Man in America*, her portrait of Benjamin Franklin, and insisted on medication just so she could fight off the pain long enough to complete the book in time for the Bicentennial. I know that Frederick Lewis Allen's genius for popular American history and culture was not appreciated by his colleagues at *Harper's*. I have learned that Harriet Beecher Stowe's *Uncle Tom's Cabin* was supposed to have been serialized in the very first issue of *The Atlantic Monthly*, but that an accident at sea prevented the plates from reaching Boston. I know where Dr. Harvey Cushing, the famous surgeon, used to live in New Haven. I have heard details about the labors of Charles Nordhoff and James Norman Hall, out in Tahiti during the 1920s, when they wrote the famous *Bounty* trilogy. I know something about the democratic interaction that used to take place on American trains, and the lucky circumstances under which Hervey Allen came to write his *Anthony Adverse*. I have held in my memory, for twelve years now, a story about Sinclair Lewis, about how he returned a publisher's weekly stipend so he could reclaim his poverty and his writing edge. I know a story about H. L. Mencken that describes his coming to Boston, during the 1920s, to sell on the Boston Common a copy of his *American Mercury* containing the "offensive" story "Hatrack," in order to challenge Boston's Watch and Ward Society, and incidentally, help win artistic freedom for D. H. Lawrence and all American writers. I know something about the debate that the Sacco-Vanzetti case set off among the faculty of the Harvard Law School, and I know something about the personal heroism of Felix Frankfurter. And I know a little bit more, in 1979, about the generous and compassionate spirit that preserved the human side of these other people.

Some facts are easily available. Edward Weeks was born in Elizabeth, New Jersey, in 1898, of English and Dutch ancestry, to an old, established American family. He grew up in the New Jersey-New York society that Edith Wharton knew intimately. He wanted to attend Princeton, but was not admitted. He entered Cornell, intending to become an engineer, but withdrew in 1917, at the American intervention in World War I, to volunteer as an ambulance driver in the French army. He returned from France in 1919 and entered Harvard College, studying English under Dean L. B. R. Briggs. He earned extra money by free-lancing for the *Boston Evening Transcript*. After graduation he worked one summer as a harvest hand in Kansas, then worked his way to England on a Scottish cattle boat. He studied at Cambridge for several terms before returning to the United States and settling in New York's Greenwich Village. There he began work as a bookseller for the new publishing firm Boni and Liveright. In 1924 he was offered a job in Boston by Ellery Sedgwick, the eighth editor of *The Atlantic Monthly*. He began as first reader, helped to publish Ernest Hemingway's first short story, and later was instrumental in reorganizing, and broadening the readership of, the Atlantic Monthly Press. In 1938, at the age of forty-one, he succeeded Ellery Sedgwick as editor in chief of *The Atlantic Monthly*. He remained editor for twenty-eight years, longer than any man in the history of the magazine, and made it into one of the most influential publications in American history and in the English-speaking world. He has lectured in almost every part of this country, has served on the Board of Overseers at Harvard, and has been a member of more committees and civic organizations than it is possible to name. He has remained extraordinarily faithful to Chautauqua, that island of calm and sincere reflection on Lake Chautaqua near Jamestown, New York; he has lectured there almost every summer for almost half a century. I have been told that he is an excellent dancer, and he is exceptionally graceful with a cane. He plays a good hand of poker. He likes to fish. In 1966 Edward Weeks retired from his editorship of *The Atlantic Monthly* and became senior editor of the Atlantic Monthly Press. He still edits books.

These are the biographical facts, but they supply only the outline of a career. They are insufficient to define the man. Edward Weeks can be best understood in relation to an institution and in terms of his elaboration of its guiding premise. James Russell Lowell, the first editor of *The Atlantic*, pledged to create an indigenously *American* magazine, "free without being fanatical," one that would open its pages to "all available talents of all shades of opinion." To make good on such a pledge, the editor himself would have to be committed to a strict regime of personal growth. If he is not to become the prisoner of his charge, he must constantly remain a few steps ahead of it, and ahead of its audience, in order to feed the new parts of himself into the institution and from there into the thinking of his readers. He must continually re-create an institution in terms of a constantly growing self, and that self must be consistently conscious of what is taking place in the world. This can become a killing pace and a wearying process, because the man must be committed to change as the dominant norm. There are very few people equipped psychologically or physically to assimilate the rapidly accelerating flow of events that has characterized this century. But when the records of this century are examined, when the writers who come after us try to discover what people thought and felt and tried to be, their loves and fears and moral concerns, their small triumphs and larger defeats, there will be no better record available than the one preserved by the institution in Boston headed, for twenty-eight eventful years, by Edward Weeks.

The names of his contributors read like a listing of the major influences on American and European literature, politics, and journalism for most of this century: André Malraux, Walter Lippmann, Felix Frankfurter, Carl

Jung, Archibald MacLeish, Edmund Wilson, Joseph Henry Jackson, C. L. Sulzberger, Joseph P. Kennedy, Jean-Paul Sartre, David Riesman, Gilbert Seldes, John Steinbeck, Ernest Hemingway, Richard Wright, Virginia Woolf, Theodore Roethke, John Cheever, William Saroyan, Geoffrey Household, Oscar Lewis, George Bernard Shaw, William Butler Yeats, Alexander Woollcott, Martin Luther King, Jr. The names are too many to list to completion.

Edward Weeks built the magazine out of his own personality, and he broadened that personality with the times. In a word, he "personalized" an institution, encouraging it, and its readership, to follow his lead. He led his readers everywhere, without forgetting who he was or the premise he was attempting to elaborate. He was successful, and he knew it. This, perhaps, was the source of the calm authority in his voice. Beneath the words, no matter what the occasion, was the assurance of a man who had already been there, seen things, weighed them in the balance, and was patient in his belief that people would eventually catch up with him. Perhaps it was for this reason that his monthly book-review column was called "The Peripatetic Reviewer." The word *peripatetic* means, according to one dictionary, "in the manner of Aristotle, who walked around while teaching philosophy in the Lyceum of ancient Athens." Edward Weeks's reviews always tested the books under consideration against his own experience. That experience had been broad enough, and rich enough, to encourage a personal standard of judgment. The fact that during his long tenure the magazine had a tremendous increase in influence and circulation is a practical testimony to the trust its readers placed in his experience and judgment. He signed all his letters "Sincerely as ever," and there are probably few people who would doubt the truth of this.

IV

A friend in Virginia, an excellent writer named Peter Taylor, told me a story about a conversation he once had with Robert Frost. "Taylor," the poet had boomed at him, "there are only two states, Massachusetts and Virginia, Massachusetts and Virginia!" Frost must have intended this comment in a very special sense: the influence these two commonwealths have had on the development of the American continent and the American character. They are the oldest English-speaking regions of the country. They were founded less than a decade apart. Both contributed basic documents to the American tradition: John Winthrop's sermon, in 1630, defining the spiritual meaning of the American adventure, and Thomas Jefferson's Declaration, in 1776, establishing, on paper at least, a new American identity. Both commonwealths, after inventing the country, supplied the men and the ideas that took it apart again. In that war both commonwealths lost many of its best sons. But in that great, unfinished effort to reconstruct the country, Massachusetts, for a long time, stood virtually alone. There were the moral resources left behind by the Puritans and then those of the abolitionists, there were the colleges and universities in Cambridge and Boston, and there were the personal memories of those who knew what the war had been about, and why so many young men had died.

At one time Boston was called the Athens of America. It was never really this, but its rich traditions did attract idealists and intellectuals from all parts of the country. They became immersed in these traditions, and tended to carry them as far as their idealism and energies would permit. Boston has always been a place where ideas are debated and exchanged. It has always been a place where independence is valued, even at the considerable price— as in opposition to the Mexican War in 1848 and to the reelection of Richard Nixon in 1972—of standing alone. With its universities and publishing houses, its independent people and rich traditions, Boston was a haven. But there is a subtle danger in becoming sui generis. The people who come into such places and find them comfortable sometimes adapt their personalities to the dominant style and pass into a pleasant kind of obscurity. They become stylized. It requires extraordinary strength of character, or an iron will, to prevent this subtle process from taking place.

Edward Weeks came to Boston from suburban New Jersey and New York City. He came after a considerable apprenticeship in the more practical aspects of publishing. As a bookseller, walking the streets of New York, he learned how books moved *after* they were written and edited and published. He also learned about the country by moving through it, experiencing its diversity on trains, by lecturing before clubs and civic groups, by teaching at Yaddo and Bread Loaf, by getting to know the writers who wrote the books and the kinds of people who read them. By doing this he brought the rest of the country to Boston with him; and after becoming editor of *The*

Atlantic Monthly he continued to be aware, and to make his readers aware, that he and they were part of a national and international community.

But Edward Weeks also took special pains to encourage unknown writers, to take chances in order to grow in his own understanding. Under his direction, the Atlantic Monthly Press solicited over-the-transom submissions, and this ongoing tradition, over the years, has helped to launch writers as different as Mazo de la Roche, Geoffrey Household, and Joseph Wambaugh.

At his encouragement, Agnes Newton Keith, an American woman in Borneo, wrote *Three Came Home*, an account of her family's survival of a Japanese concentration camp during World War II. He also encouraged Ved Mehta, an Indian, to write *Face to Face*, an account of his triumph over blindness. At Edward Weeks's suggestion, DeWitt Wallace, publisher of *The Reader's Digest*, sponsored a writing contest for students attending the United Negro College Fund colleges. In 1963, long before Martin Luther King became a nationally known spokesman, Weeks published in *The Atlantic Monthly* King's eloquent "Letter from a Birmingham Jail."

But his greatest love is fishing, for both new writers and salmon. He has fished streams and rivers in all parts of the United States, in Canada, England, Holland, Russia, Iceland, and Slovenia. He has cultivated a graciousness in this: he always throws the little fish, writers or grilse, back into the stream to give them time to grow. But he loves to catch a salmon with fight in it. At dinner parties at his home on Beacon Hill, especially in the summer, guests are sometimes treated to fresh salmon he has caught himself and had shipped back to Boston from Canada or from as far away as Iceland. He tells stories about his fishing expeditions that always include references to people he remembers fondly, from local guides to college presidents, from French Canadian backwoodsmen and Russian peasants to diplomats. He is always listening, always learning, always looking at events from the personal point of view. In *Fresh Waters*, his account of his various fishing expeditions, there are, beneath the peripatetic treatment of fishing as an art, very serious discussions of ecology, the nature of the American character, U.S.-Soviet relations, biology, the more practical aspects of publishing, and much more. The book is also an account of friends made, travels undertaken. *Fresh Waters* begins with a small pond in Boston, and takes the reader to rivers and streams and people over a good third of the earth. It is not a fish story.

Edward Weeks is gifted with a natural, sympathetic curiosity. This trait is part of what has made him such an outstanding editor. Where another editor might be tempted to lapse into convenient silence with an author, or retreat into the more comfortable perspective provided by a stereotype, he demands direct experience. Once, in the late sixties, there was a highly publicized picture of black students at Cornell marching, armed, out of a campus dormitory. At lunch, obviously concerned about the incident, he said, "James, when I was lecturing at the Negro colleges back in the fifties I noticed how frightened the students seemed. Why are they still so frightened?"

In the summer of 1968 I sent him a story about black dining-car waiters, written from their point of view, in their idiom, and I had spiced the story with some of their choicest expletives. He sent back a telegram praising the story. Then, at lunch that next week, he once again praised the story, but said he worried that readers would be bothered by those certain words. He did not object outright. Instead he said, "This is a superb story. I could hardly touch my pencil to it. Except that I have a little trouble with certain words. On page two, for example, you have this word '——' spoken twice, and on page three it appears again, along with this other word '——.' James, I think that's overdoing it a bit. I suggest a compromise. Why not take out one of the '——s' on page two and its repetition on page three, and keep that other word on page three. In other words, I'll trade you two '——s' for one '——.'"

On another occasion, ten years later, he paid me the highest tribute an editor can pay an author. I had incorporated into a story a bitter debate between a writer and an editor over what should be cut from the story and what should be left in. I was torn between my need to make a certain statement and my desire not to implicate Weeks. He made no negative comment on this aspect of the story, and was content with the realization that only the two of us, of all the readers of the story, would know that I did not have him in mind. He deferred to what I perceived to be a necessity with a graciousness and understanding I will never forget. Yet he could be severe when he felt I was in the wrong, and he reprimanded, albeit in gentle ways. "My Christmas wish for you," he wrote one December, "is that you learn again to be more understanding." And when, at another time, I had lapsed into silence, his letter said, "If I had your talents, I would use them." But he signed both letters "Sincerely as ever," and I have no doubt that he meant it both times.

As an editor he was comparable to Maxwell Perkins, whom he knew personally. Both men came of age during the gentleman's era of American publishing. Perkins will be remembered because he edited the books of Ernest Hemingway, F. Scott Fitzgerald, and Thomas Wolfe. Edward Weeks will be remembered because he maintained that gentlemanly tradition further into the twentieth century than any man alive. But he also went looking for talent, in both his personal travels and in the special attention *The Atlantic* gave unpublished writers. Edward Weeks knew that talent could be found in the most unlikely places—a Japanese prison camp in Borneo, a small village in Canada, or the backwoods of Tennessee. Maxwell Perkins could sit in New York and let writers of genius come to him. Edward Weeks went out fishing for them. He cultivated people who told stories, good stories, and who knew how to look at the world in personal terms.

He edited many books that became best sellers, even though they were not edited to appeal to a mass audience. They began as good stories, and he edited them to be even clearer, sharper stories. He had a clear eye for dramatic detail, could project himself into the minds of both the writer and his characters, and so had sympathy for the story being developed. Always in his own experience there was some memory, some personal bridge into the writer's sense of story. He made meticulous notes, had a draftsman's sense of design, never patronized his writers, and, if necessary, fought for them. Many of the books he edited are now out of print, but many others are ageless: the *Bounty* trilogy, Ralph McGill's *The South and the Southerner*, the early stories of Joyce Carol Oates, Samuel Eliot Morison's *Admiral of the Ocean Sea* and fifteen-volume *History of the United States Naval Operations in World War Two*, the novels of Edith Sitwell, the forthcoming biography of Walter Lippmann, the books of the American historian Oscar Handlin.

VI

In 1974, at the age of seventy-six, Edward Weeks returned to Chautauqua to present the keynote speech at the institution's centennial celebration. His audience numbered in the thousands. He returned with special pleasure, he told them, because it was at Chautauqua that he had met and courted his first wife, fifty-two years before. His speech was entitled "American Writers Come of Age," and in it he traced the development of the American language from Melville and Whitman and Twain through the best American writers of the twentieth century. He also stated the guiding premise of *The Atlantic Monthly*, as formulated by its first editor, James Russell Lowell, and as elaborated by Edward Weeks well into the twentieth century. There was no need to be specific about his own work. His personality and the strict attention of his audience were sufficient evidence that it had been well done. He spoke to an audience of old friends, people who had followed the lead of his voice for almost half a century. He stood in a huge amphitheater, under the summer sky, and used his voice like a fine-tuned, eloquent musical instrument. He told his audience what he believed, not what he thought they wanted to hear. His speech was optimistic, during that bleak, uncertain time, in its assurance that Lowell's premise would continue being elaborated.

He began his story in Boston, with the efforts of Ralph Waldo Emerson to break American literature away from its paternalistic tie to England, and quoted Emerson's response, while in England, to a condescending Thomas Carlyle: "I like the English. They are as good as they are handsome. But I surely know that as soon as I return to Massachusetts I shall lapse at once into the feeling that I know the geography of America inevitably inspires: that we play the game with immense advantage, that *there* and not here is the seat and center of the British race, and that England, an old and exhausted island, must one day be contented like other parents to be strong only in her children."

Weeks spoke for American literature: "What Mark Twain neglected to tell us was this truth: that the size of our country and the flexibility of our democracy impelled American writers to tackle subjects of wide-ranging geographic scale which were completely different from the quietly controlled, permanently stratified literature of England."

He spoke of the changes that had taken place during this century, of the influx of immigrants from every country on earth and of the growth of an American language, which incorporated all their idioms. He spoke about the health of this: "No other country had ever ventured on an experiment like this. It made us the most heterogeneous nation in the world. But the Anglo-

88   A BOOK FOR BOSTON

Saxon purists among us did not approve." He cited John Jay Chapman, Owen Wister. He called Henry James "that fastidious, not to say fussy, bachelor."

And Weeks spoke of his hopes for the country and its literature: "I regard these changes as milestones on our way to a multiracial society. I think our country is too large for a single literary capital. Good writing is just as likely to come from Mississippi as it is from San Francisco or Boulder, Colorado, or Peterborough, New Hampshire. It is my hope for the future that we who are readers and critics will avoid the exclusiveness and patronage of the English that so irritated James Russell Lowell a century ago. It is my hope that we will keep listening, keep *listening* for those stories and poems and novels that are sure to come from the fusion of our bloods."

A lady in Ohio told me that two very significant things occurred during Weeks's stay at Chautauqua. After a long day of speechmaking, when he was resting, someone mentioned to him that some of the people did not understand anything about black Americans and what they wanted. "Oh, is that all?" he said. "That's easy. I'll tell them." And he got back on the platform and gave a second lecture. At another point, while recalling some of the stories he had recorded in his autobiography, *My Green Age*, he spoke of the many young men who had died during the Second World War. He lost his composure and cried. But on another occasion, during a subsequent visit, there was a happier moment that resulted from the war. Agnes Newton Keith, whom Weeks had encouraged to write about her Japanese prison-camp experience, came to Chautauqua to lecture. I was shown a picture of the two of them, seated on the front porch of one of those large, imposing Victorian houses. The lady, still suffering from the effects of the physical tortures she had undergone, was smiling proudly along with the man.

VII

I have always called him "Mr. Weeks," partly in deference to his age, but mostly because, in his presence, I am aware that he contains legions. Once, in Baltimore, when he had come for a short visit on his way to Washington to attend the funeral of a friend, I drove him to the Penn Station. The train was due in a few minutes and I took his old-fashioned leather bags out of my car and was about to carry them into the station for him. It was a sentimental mistake, the kind that only a young man is likely to make. "I'll take my bags," he said curtly. And he stood there for a moment, ramrod stiff and impeccable in his three-piece summer suit and starched white shirt and handcrafted tie. Then he walked briskly with the bags into the station. Seeing a redcap, he said, "What time's the next train, Captain?"

I have heard that he has experienced great tragedies in his personal life. He has never talked about them.

Edward Weeks is a traveling man, a keen fisherman, who has learned his own way around the country. He knows he is not British, although his voice has incorporated the fine music of cultivated British speech. He knows he is not really a Boston Brahmin, even though he has accepted and elaborated beautifully the literary premise of that city. He is from Elizabeth, New Jersey, the battlefields of France, Harvard College, the wheatfields of Kansas, the cultivation of Cambridge, England, the streets and bookstores of New York, and the traditions of both Chautauqua and Boston. He was born into the American upper class and he has honored the best of its traditions. Not content, however, with the security and insulation provided by this advantage, he has gone out into the country, fishing for salmon and stories, and has brought the best of both back to Boston with him. He has re-created himself continuously through this process, feeding the newest parts of himself through an institution and giving himself back to the world. This has been a gesture of epic proportions, and he has survived long enough to tell a great part of our century's story, in very personal terms.

Many books and countless memories will survive Edward Weeks. There is a Latin phrase, the epitaph of the English architect Christopher Wren, inscribed on his most famous building, St. Paul's Cathedral in London: *Si monumentum requiris, circumspice:* "If you seek his monument, look around you." Edward Weeks has special connections in England, but in elaborating his personal premise and in re-creating himself, he has become as American as anyone in this turbulent century is likely to become.

View of State Street, 1976. NICHOLAS NIXON

Mid-19th century engraving commemorating "The First Musical Festival in New England, King's Chapel, Boston," on January 10, 1786. MASSACHUSETTS HISTORICAL SOCIETY

OPPOSITE: The Boston Arena on St. Botolph Street, 1930. Photograph by Berenice Abbott. BOSTON ATHENAEUM

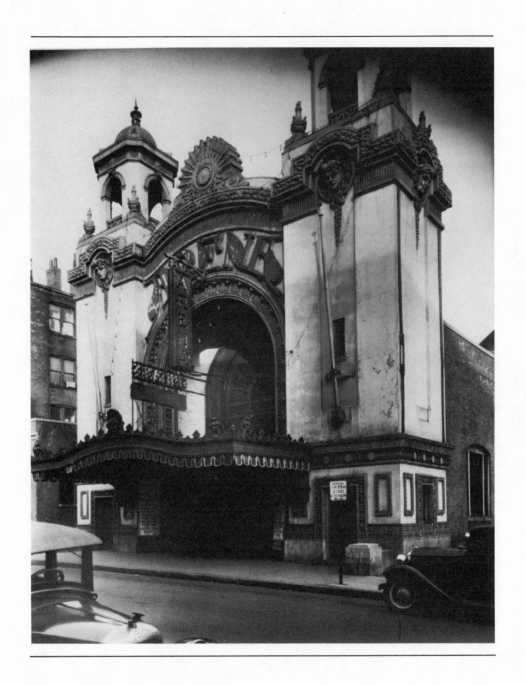

Arthur Fiedler directing the Copley Christmas Choral Cavalry, 1975. COPLEY PLAZA HOTEL

OPPOSITE: Elma Lewis, 1971. LYNN MCLAREN

Serge Koussevitzky, by Alfred A. Knopf (from the book Sixty Photographs by Alfred A. Knopf, © 1975). ALFRED A. KNOPF, INC.

OPPOSITE: *Sarah Caldwell, 1970.* LYNN MCLAREN

Opera Company of Boston

"The most exciting venture of its kind in the country". Life Magazine

season '70

sarah caldwell, artistic director
ruth capers mckay, executive director

The Flying Dutchman
wagner

The dramatic saga of the legendary seaman, his tormented love and
inevitable encounter with destiny.

Wed. Jan 28   Fri. Jan. 30   Sun. Feb. 1 (Mat.)

The Daughter of the Regiment
donizetti

Delight in the absurd, gay dilemma of a coluratura waif found on the battlefield
and adopted by an entire regiment

Sat. Feb. 21   Mon. Feb. 23

The Good Soldier Schweik
kurka

Applaud the hilarious adventures of the non-hero of Hasek's famous novel.
"A powerful, hilarious, needling, absurd three-penny epic". NEW YORK TIMES

Fri. Apr. 3   Sun. Apr. 5 (Mat.)

The Fisherman and His Wife
updike-schuller

The world premiere of an opera fable for children of all ages. Commissioned by
the Junior League of Boston for performance by The Opera Company of Boston.
words by john updike · music by gunther schuller

Fri. May 8   Sun. May 10 (Mat.)

Rigoletto
verdi

A lyrical melodrama of love, dishonor, vendetta, and ultimate tragedy.

Wed. June 3   Fri. June 5   Sun. June 7 (Mat.)

eunice alberts   vern shinall
john alexander   beverly sills
carole bogard   thomas stewart
donald gramm   giorgio tozzi
mac morgan   benita valente

phyllis curtin

in Boston at the Savoy Theatre   in Cambridge at M.

Tickets   267-8   172 Newbury St.   Bost

Advertisement for Charles A. Smith & Co., tailors, showing the Old State House as a mercantile building. Mid-19th century lithograph by Tappan & Bradford. BOSTON ATHENAEUM

A Sure Thing on State Street

You never know Boston until you have dealt with her money. You can walk her streets and visit her monuments: Old Ironsides, Beacon and Bunker hills, Paul Revere's house, the Old North Church. You can eat in her best restaurants: Locke-Ober's, the Ritz, Maison Robert. You can live in Boston all your life and feel that you are surrounded by dead history, by Puritan attitudes that reflect rigidity and tired conservative principles. But though an outsider's impression of Boston may be of a cold tradition, of closed doors that will never be open, the facts are otherwise.

It is alleged that when Mrs. Pusey first came to Boston with her husband, Nathan, Harvard's twenty-fourth president, she was invited to a reception in the Back Bay. Mrs. Pusey commented to several dowagers, "Oh, everyone has been so wonderful to us. Everyone has been so kind and generous."

"It's obvious, Mrs. Pusey," one of the Boston dowagers said to her, "that you have not met any of the *right* people."

We secretly relish this facade of cold-roast Boston. But we know that the real truth is that Boston is many things. She is high technology: Raytheon, Polaroid, Ionics, Wang Laboratories. She is Digital Equipment and Data General, the two largest manufacturers of minicomputers in the world. She is General Cinema and Stop and Shop. She is Child World. She is Gillette. Boston is a true heavyweight money manager of billions of dollars of pension and private assets, where entire offices exist solely to invest the funds of a single family's fortune. Boston is the only city in America where law firms commonly run their own trust departments, several of them controlling capital pools of more than half a billion. The smartest money in the world has sought

Boston management for more than one hundred years. What is not generally appreciated is that the money flows here not merely to be preserved, but to *grow*. Money flows here in the expectation that it will multiply.

I'm lucky. I can sit in my boardroom, that mirror of the soul, and know that the action and the information will rub off on me. Perhaps a recent day in Boston will tell you what I mean.

The wind and rain blow up State Street from the harbor, as if daring anyone to venture out. It is the kind of day when the Squire often visits. The Squire loves days that challenge the pedestrian. He is in his midsixties, straight as a stick, and accustomed to being obeyed. The Squire wears old-fashioned slip-on rubbers, an ancient Burberry from Jermyn Street, and a felt hat with the snap brim turned down that was new when Albie Booth played against Harvard in 1932.

"You know why I come out on days like this?" he asks me. "Because no one else comes out. People break appointments in rotten weather. That leaves people free to pay attention to *me*."

He slaps his hat against his leg, shaking the moisture onto the floor. "There are a lot of old customs," the Squire says, "that should not have disappeared. One of them is the hat. Every man looks good in a hat—bald men, skinny men, fat men, ugly men. Hats keep the rain and snow off in winter, the sun off in summer. And, if you are practical enough to wear a hat, you can afford to cross over the line in other ways."

"Meaning what?"

"Meaning buy me ten thousand shares of Actual Devices at forty-three and a half or better."

Bang! You think you're getting stodgy old Boston. But the truth is that the Squire has only one concern: keep the money building, make it grow, and—if circumstances seem propitious—take a reasonable chance to make an extraordinary return.

"You must remember how we in Boston regard money," the Squire says. "Money is holy, a sign of election, if you have read your Calvin. It isn't something that happens by accident or merely because you've worked hard for it. It is a symbol, a vehicle . . ."

The Squire watches the ticker tape until he sees his trade going by, ten thousand shares of Actual Devices at forty-three and a half.

"I'll tell you, because you listen pretty well," he said. "I'm buying this stock because my good friend Parker tells me that a German company is going to offer better than seventy per share for the stock. Parker is the fellow to catch at lunch. If I'm at the club and Parker is there, on his third martini, he'll let you in on secrets. And Parker always knows."

"When you get rid of the odd-lotter, let me know," booms a voice from outside my office, and in walks Lou the Shooter, fresh from spending five thousand dollars on four suits, five pair of shoes, and a half-dozen cashmere sweaters. Lou the Shooter is only kidding about getting rid of the Squire. They have met before in my office and the Squire doesn't seem to mind Lou's manner. Which is generally insulting and bombastic. "Get them before they get you," Lou is fond of saying. It is a strategy that has worked well for him. Lou wants everyone to know that he has *spent* more money in the last few years than most people earn in a lifetime. A few years ago, Lou the Shooter sold a discount toy operation to a big-board conglomerate. His personal share of the sale was 3.4 million, and he still carries in his wallet a Xeroxed copy of the underwriter's check to prove it. Often at a bar or in a restaurant, after receiving the bill, Lou the Shooter will give the Xeroxed copy of the 3.4-million-dollar check to the waiter. "Can you cash this?" he will say. That's Lou the Shooter.

"That is a classy gentleman," the Squire said to me sarcastically after first meeting Lou. "Remind me to take my business back to Goldman Sachs."

Snug in my office this rainy day, Lou the Shooter starts right in on the Squire. "Why don't you dress up your act?" Lou demands. "Get some new clothes. The Spanish-American War is over. What did you come in here for, some self-addressed stamped envelopes? A quote on General Motors? Here," Lou says to me. "Buy me a thousand Portia Electric. Now *there's* an order, ten thousand bucks at a whack."

The Squire stands up, towering over Lou the Shooter (who has a permanent stoop from years of leaning over benches, repairing kids' toys before he hit the jackpot).

"Do you consider yourself a Bostonian?" the Squire asks.

"Hell, yes. I've been here seven years. I don't even root for the Yankees anymore."

"Then I'm going to give you a history lesson."

The Squire insists that Lou the Shooter put on his raincoat with all the epaulets and brass rings. "You think you've just invented speculation?" the Squire asks Lou. "Let me show you about money."

I grab my coat also and go with them, convinced that I am about to lose two clients. In the elevator the Squire says, "Everyone who ever made a lot of money fast thinks that *he* is the only person to have experienced that phenomenon. An understandable belief. But I want to prove to you that old Boston money has its roots in *adventure*, not conservatism. And I'll bet you a bottle of nineteen-fifty-three Cheval Blanc that we're just as venturesome *now* as we ever were before."

"You've got yourself a bet," says Lou the Shooter, who only drinks champagne cocktails and figures the Squire is letting himself off cheap.

We walk in the rain to the waterfront while the Squire tells us about privateers who minted coin during the Revolution and the War of 1812, about the China traders and how Bostonians opened up the Orient and the Hawaiian Islands. He tells us about fortunes made and lost upon the sea. The Squire speaks of Lowell and Lawrence—the families, the cities, and the mills they built.

"The Ames family," he says, "not only financed and controlled the Union Pacific Railroad, they had the foresight to back the genius Steinmetz, whose work led to the founding of General Electric. The Forbes family bankrolled Alexander Graham Bell and were the prime movers behind what became American Telephone and Telegraph. Oh, Boston has shooters of her own. She doesn't wave them in your face. But she's got them."

We walk up Congress Street toward State Street, Lou the Shooter taking almost two steps for every long stride of the Squire's. "But the innovation and daring don't stop with the nineteenth century," the Squire goes on. "We went from dominating the wool trade into backing the beginnings of space technology. We funded Polaroid and the golden computer belt on Route 128. We devised and built the first industrial parks, the first modern shopping center, even the first twin movie theaters. Modern venture-capital techniques were born in Boston with General Doriot and American Research and Development. And we can't forget our innovations and dominance in money management—Paul Cabot and the rise of the modern mutual fund, Massachusetts Investors Trust, and Mr. Johnson at Fidelity Management. We even bankrolled the Big Mac. But I'm going to show you the key to understanding our approach to money."

The Squire pauses and looks up. The rain has stopped and the sun is beginning to squeeze around high clouds. "Right on time," the Squire says. Good Bostonians know the sea, and they know the weather.

"Predicting rain don't get you a bottle of wine," Lou the Shooter mutters, chastened somewhat by the Squire's revelations.

"Come," the Squire commands, and we walk into a bank, a bank that had its beginning at that site in 1792. We walk over a flagstone floor, bordered by wall paneling of Michigan pine and English oak. "This is Boston, too," the Squire says, leading us to a corner where the office of Allan Forbes still stands, preserved as if it were from a countinghouse of the seventeenth and eighteenth centuries. Ships' models sit on shelves; whaling prints and watercolors line the walls. Through the small-paned windows we can see the towers of State Street, the boldly modern City Hall, and the cobbles that lead to Faneuil Hall (which is simultaneously the oldest and the newest marketing wonder of America). "Several more things," the Squire says to Lou the Shooter. "You bought one thousand shares of some stock this morning."

"I told you," Lou snaps.

"Show Lou my slip," the Squire asks me. Silently, I produce the buy order for ten thousand shares of stock, selling at forty-three and a half per share. Lou the Shooter gulps.

We walk from the bank into brilliant sunshine. The breeze from the sea is brisk. It makes one feel like working. We pause on State Street, which used to be King Street before 1776. "One more thing," the Squire says. We all look up the street away from the harbor. Outlined against the sky is the massive tower of One Boston Place, the skyscraper that houses the managers of billions of dollars of assets from around the world. Its bulk and mirrored surface form a striking backdrop for the old brick State House, sitting beneath the towers and looking just as solid as its newer brethren. The old State House, topped by the carved lion and unicorn, casts its own small but solid shadow upon the plaque that marks the site of the Boston Massacre. "That's Boston," the Squire says. "The contrast. The old and the new."

Traffic moves up State Street, building toward the rush hour. We see a small truck go past. Holding on to the tailgate is a young man. He looks the very image of a new-breed investment banker or lawyer: his hair cut long and carefully parted in the middle, he wears a three-piece suit and highly polished black wing-tipped shoes of English leather. His feet rest on a skate board, and the truck is pulling him along at a nice clip. The young man waves at us as we stare in disbelief. "Never doubt what lies beneath the surface of Bostonians," the Squire says. "It's the energy and the daring. The willingness to take chances."

"I don't believe what I just saw," says Lou the Shooter. "A banker hitching a ride on a skate board."

"Believe it," said the Squire. "That was my grandson."

Lou is pleased that a liquor store nearby has a bottle of 1953 Cheval Blanc. And it set him back only eighty-three dollars and thirty-three cents.

Sign of H. Cabot, painter, 1833. THE BOSTON SOCIETY

Fireflies

Boots Farnham loved his daughter, Jenny, more even than he loved Celia.

Celia Bourne was a pretty, soft-spoken, intelligent woman whom he'd met in the library at Boston University on a cold Tuesday in January of 1969. She was twenty then, a voice major in her last year. Singing was everything to her until she met Boots. She was from South Boston, but her parents were immigrants from Wicklow and Belfast, and she had been raised by her mother to be a singer in the traditional Celtic style. Celia's teachers had low regard for what they considered ethnic singing, and, while she was up to the Italian operatic manner, she preferred the simple directness of Gaelic and Elizabethan music. The best she would say of B.U. was that it was there she learned to accompany herself on the harp.

But in one way at least Celia's teachers were right. It takes more to make a career than a pure tone, a simplicity of spirit, and a repertoire of obscure ballads. She graduated, but not with honors and not with the slightest prospect of making a living at singing. She got a job selling clothes at the Ann Taylor in Harvard Square. She had that slender, hard body like a boy's that chic clothes required.

Boots Farnham had not thought Celia the most beautiful woman he'd ever seen, but he liked looking at her from the beginning. He'd choked on his pipe smoke that Tuesday in the reading room when she approached him confidently and asked him why he was staring at her. He'd blushed and denied that he was and then, despite his fluster, he'd asked her to have coffee with him.

He was twenty-six then. For another year he continued taking courses toward his doctorate in philosophy and taught undergraduates the difference between Husserl and Heidegger. But Farnham had no real gift for philosophy; certainly he had no gift for analytical American philosophy. At the end of 1969 he quit, deciding finally that he was not smart enough to do what his father had done—make a career out of thinking. The simple acts of resigning his grants and withdrawing from graduate school, accomplished by the most mundane filing of forms, were in fact momentous deeds for him, which might have occasioned celebration as signals of his freedom were they not humiliating for being so long overdue. He had never before made such choices according to his own lights and not his father's.

Francis Farnham senior was professor emeritus of philosophy at George Washington University in Washington, where Boots had grown up. He admired his father, who, as a philosopher, was more European than American and whose reputation as an interpreter of the existentialists was well established. (In fact, his epistemology of freedom was a popular college textbook and it was entitled *The Phenomenology of Ethics*.)

Boots was Francis Farnham junior, an only child. He got his nickname from the fact that for a time as a boy he'd worn metal leg braces to correct the pronounced limp a year-long case of polio had left him with. He was four when he got his first leg braces, and he was the one who dispelled his parents' qualms by calling them boots. The name stuck, and he didn't mind it until he was twelve, when the limp was less severe but still noticeable. By then, though, he wasn't wearing braces and only his oldest friends connected his limp to his name. In fact, he came to like "Boots" better than "Frank," which is what everyone called his father; a strange name, he would think much later, for a philosopher. But then, of course, not so strange for a philosopher as "Boots" would have been.

Professor Farnham was cruelly disappointed when Boots left graduate school, and angrily accused him of wasting his mind. But Boots knew that his father was at least as disappointed in himself, that his retirement had cut him from his moorings and broken his will to write. Boots's mind? He was afraid of wasting his own mind. Boots took the old man's complaints in stride. What he was more interested in was Celia.

Boots's limp was gone by the time he met Celia. Other scars remained. His calf muscles had never fully developed. He hated taking his clothes off in front of anyone. With women the process had been inexpressibly painful to him. That shyness threatened Boots anew the first night that he and Celia spent together. If they'd met in the summer he could have gone to the beach with her first, to prepare her. As it was, he guessed that she had no idea that his legs were, as he thought of them, misshapen. When he took his trousers off that night in her apartment in Brighton she looked right at his legs and she grimaced as he'd been afraid she would and she stooped to touch them. When she looked up at him she said she wanted to know about it but not right then, and she drew him down.

Boots Farnham was changed by Celia Bourne. He took more pleasure in everything because of her. He told stories with a verve and wit that were new and wholly uncharacteristic. He began walking a lot from his place to hers, and then along the esplanade of the Charles, sometimes without her, and he began to feel much more vigorous for the exercise. He loved the toy-land quality of the river basin when the sailboats were out, snapping at the wind and crisscrossing against the blue Cambridge sky.

Boots also began playing the piano again. Celia had a fourth-hand Steinway in her apartment, the most beautifully toned instrument he had ever played, though she was sure the sounding board was cracked. Celia let him accompany her on easy American pieces, but her serious practicing she still did at her harp in private. Gradually she taught him traditional Gaelic tunes, and he proved adept at improvising accompaniments. They did very well together, and not just at music.

It was Celia who suggested they move in together, which they did in May of 1970. Celia found an elegant little apartment on the first floor of an old brownstone on Bay State Road. The rear window looked out on the Charles, and the main room was large enough for the piano. By the time they'd lived there a year Boots could not imagine that he had ever lived without her, or ever would again. That was when he asked her to marry him. When she said she would an enormous relief came over him, as if, without knowing it, he'd been holding his breath for all twenty-eight years of his life, and now was breathing freely for the first time.

Once he admitted that he did not want to be a philosopher it was obvious to him what he would do. Working with wood had been his passion, even as a kid. He had spent all his spare time as a boy working in old Mr. Sanborn's cabinet shop on P Street in Georgetown. Boots had earned money toward his undergraduate tuition refinishing antiques. He loved not just working with wood, but working with old wood, and he thought he might be good enough to start his own shop. Celia encouraged him and that is what he did.

He set up in the small barn behind the house they bought on Rockview Street in Jamaica Plain. J.P. had once been a farming town and then a flourishing suburb and was now a part of the city remarkable for its fine old houses and for the diversity of its people. Their house was one of the more modest ones, but they couldn't have afforded even it without the SBA loan Boots obtained for his shop. On her own initiative Celia had a business card printed for him and sent out an announcement to area tradesmen and neighbors and placed ads in local papers—all of which surprised and delighted Boots. That was how it began that Celia handled the business end of things, sending out the bills each month and ordering stock and keeping her husband's jobs on a proper schedule. Without Celia, Farnham wouldn't have known what to charge his customers, or even when to charge them.

After seven years he had more customers than he could properly serve. He had developed as a specialty the repair and restoration of nineteenth-century furniture of the sort found in old sea-captains' houses, which abounded north and south of Boston. He even did restoration work for museums and historical societies.

Jenny was born on January 19, 1973. She weighed seven pounds, four ounces. She had fierce red hair, as he did. Her dark eyes were jewels, her own in every way. Jenny learned to walk as if expressly for the purpose of plunging down the slight hill behind the house to find her father where she knew he'd be, bent over his lathe, turning a piece of oak. He worked with his felt hat on, and Jenny always insisted that he take it off when she came in and put it on her head. He tried to understand why she was so special to him. She was such a dramatic mark, for one thing, on the line of his life. Before Jenny, everything was so much more abstract, so much more public, so much more hasty and—yes—shallow.

But that was because, before Jenny, everything took its meaning from Vietnam. Boots and Celia were typical of their generation in Boston, taking for granted throughout their school days the profoundly melancholy weight of that war. The first Christmas Celia and Boots celebrated in Jamaica Plain (less than a month before Jenny's birth) was, for example, the Christmas of the bombing of Hanoi. Boots was stunned by the reports of the blind American brutality. He was shocked at what his country was doing and shocked, equally, at how angry it made him. Neither Boots nor Celia had ever been anything like radicals, but the Christmas bombing affected them both. It made them wonder if they were doing something wrong by starting their own life together. Were they like the bleary-eyed kids who'd fled to the country when it was clear the world, having been given fair notice, was not going to change its ways for them?

Farnham hated to think of himself as a romantic revivalist, a pseudo-carpenter, an intellectual individualist in quest of self-fulfillment. Farnham didn't believe in self-fulfillment. He insisted to himself that he was not a narcissist, a privatist, an academic manqué. He simply wanted to be a cabinet-maker. Celia wanted to make music. They wanted to make a family. He and Celia had not abandoned their social ties or their city or their ideals. They wanted a life built on traditional New England values: good craftsmanship, neighborliness, thrift, discipline, hard work.

What nagged at him was the burdensome guilt peculiar to the draft-exempt, the boy-clergy and the 4-F like himself. And Celia was troubled partly because her best friend from Cardinal Cushing High was a Quincy girl named Annie O'Hara who'd gone to prison in 1970 for burning draft files with a priest. Celia wrote regularly to Annie at the Federal Prison for Women in Alderson, West Virginia, and talked occasionally of driving the VW down to visit her. The night before Christmas that year, when the eleven-o'clock news came on and the U.S. was still pounding Hanoi with bombs from B-52s and there were reports that the Bach Mai hospital had been blown up, Celia got up from the rocker and crossed to the couch to lie down with Boots. She put his hands on her belly to feel their baby there—his hands reassured her so—and then she put her head on his chest and cried softly. After a while she fell asleep. Boots slid away from her, turned off the TV set, and put the tree lights out. He poured himself a gin, went into the kitchen, and sat at the white enamel table. He wanted to be alone. He felt sick; he no longer wanted to be an American.

On Christmas morning the baby kicked Celia so sharply that she woke. In the kitchen she found Boots looking very white, sitting at the table with his brown felt hat on. She had never seen him so drunk and it frightened her. But then, almost as if the bombing had done it, the cease-fire was signed a month later and the American part of the war was over. That same week Nixon was inaugurated again and poor old Lyndon Johnson died and Boots turned thirty and—lo and behold!—Celia had her baby, that wonderful, perfect marshmallow of a Jenny. And why shouldn't Farnham have thought her a gift from God's own fingers?

Jenny's first trip outside the house (visits to the pediatrician excepted) was on a cool spring evening, a trip to Harvard Square. Celia had been invited by an old B.U. classmate to sing two traditional songs at a May Day festival at Passim, a coffeehouse behind the Coop. Celia sang wonderfully, and the small audience seemed to like her, though the hit of the evening was a Bluegrass duo and, frankly, Celia left wondering why she'd been included, since all the other numbers were American folk. Performing for strangers always depressed her and made her feel that her tastes were too esoteric and that she had wasted her time concentrating on Gaelic music, which was too difficult to sing well enough anyway. When they left Passim at midnight Boots carried their sleeping Jenny in her sling at his chest and led Celia over to the Cambridge Common. He took Celia into his arms and made her lie down with him and held her and Jenny both for the longest time. They looked up at the stars and didn't speak until finally Celia said, "Thanks, Babe."

That summer Boots tried teaching Jenny how to talk. Holding her in his arms, sitting on the old porch swing in front of the house, he leaned over her. "Love," he said. "Say what I say, 'love.'" Jenny peered up at him. "Love," he said. "Say 'love.'" Jenny gurgled. "Like 'Daddy,'" he said. "Like this. Say 'love.' Now you try it. Love." Jenny's eyes swiveled about to watch a bee. "A final time," Boots said. "Now, 'love'!" And then he convulsed, laughed, rubbed his face in his daughter's belly, which is how Celia found him when she came out with her harp to tune it.

"She can't pronounce it," Celia said, "but I think she understands." "No," Boots said, "Heidegger holds that the thing is not understood until it is articulated." And then he laughed again as he felt Jenny's hand tighten around his finger. "I guess she's just a retard," which was a cruel thing for him to say, and not at all what he'd intended. But Jenny was laughing too by then. And Jenny was not a retard.

She made all the difference in the world to him. It was as if what Celia's love could not heal in him hers could. Once when Jenny was three their red sixty-seven VW bug broke down on Commonwealth Avenue. Celia took the wheel and Jenny giggled hysterically while Boots pushed the car two blocks to the Gulf station on Granby Street. Boots had never done anything like that before, having always favored his legs. But this time, without thinking particularly, he'd hopped out and leaned into the back of the car. Jenny had her nose against the rear window and her head in his felt hat and she watched him pushing with such delighted admiration that he'd have kept it up for miles.

After that he started getting up earlier each day and driving six blocks to Jamaica Pond to run around it. In the first hours after dawn the pond was eerie and beautiful with the mist rising from it and the diffused light gently glancing off the water. The path was a mile long, not much for other joggers, but for Boots, who had never run in his life, it was a huge distance and he was always surprised that he could do it, and that none of the other early-morning runners seemed to notice the rough, uneven cadence of his stride. The first time he made it all the way around the pond without slowing to walk part of the way made him feel that he had finally ripped himself free from his old disease: all the way his feet thump-thumped against the earth while he whispered to himself, "I'm going to make it," and when he did he realized that he had just been granted his oldest wish. It was a gift from Jenny and he knew it. He resolved to run around that pond once every day for the rest of his life.

By 1978 there was nothing whatever to detract from Boots Farnham's happiness. "Happiness," his father had loved to say, quoting Erasmus, "is the wish to be what you are." That aphorism had been a watchword for Boots since he'd first understood it, and he had measured his life by it regularly.

Before Celia he had regularly found his life wanting. After Jenny he had stopped wondering altogether if he was happy. The pain of the war evaporated and Nixon was gone soon and it was possible to live lives of thorough attention to private things, smaller things. There was no pleasure to compare with, say, hand-making an oak frame with pegs—not nails—that would be worthy of an ancient oblong of leaded glass. If Boots had become a philosophy professor he'd have always wanted to teach his students that conceptual systems were of infinitely less value than the ordinary human stuff that such systems were supposed to describe. His complaint against his father and against his professors was that they seemed to believe the reverse. They were proselytizers—in what they said and in how they lived—of the abstract. That was why his professors lived lives of such unrelieved, monotonous loneliness; sadness clinging to them like chalk dust. That was why his father, whatever his intentions, had let his wife die feeling unloved and had let his son live feeling unworthy because he walked with a limp. Now Francis Farnham senior rattled around an old house in Georgetown hating it because his idea of it would not keep it clean or talk to him. Philosophers.

Boots preferred metaphysics to analysis. But he much preferred to metaphysics his workbench and his daughter and his three-fourths acre of Jamaica Plain and his customers and the least of his tools and Celia—Celia singing, if possible. Boots Farnham's family was blessed to live on Rockview Street in 1978 and he knew it and Celia knew it and Jenny, five, knew it.

One evening early in August Celia, Boots, and their best friends, Dick and Liz Dunn, were sitting in the bittersweet-orange nylon chairs in the Farnhams' backyard. Seth Dunn, eight, Jason Dunn, five, and Jenny were snagging fireflies and putting them in mason jars. Jenny was like a twilight vision, wearing a pink nightgown that swirled about her slim body as she scurried back and forth. The boys were her attendants. Everyone was barefoot, even the grownups, who let their feet stroke the grass, which was long and tough and losing its color as night came slowly.

They were drinking gin-and-tonics from old jelly glasses, except Boots, who drank his gin warm and neat. They were all a little loaded and it was very pleasant sitting, talking a bit, but not much, watching the children. Though

Boots's ankles and feet showed scars and gnarled bone from a dozen operations, he wasn't self-conscious about them with these people; still, he was the only one wearing long pants. Boots often looked at Celia, who, with her hair tied back with a stern black ribbon, looked like a Puritan lady. He loved to sit and look at her like that, her pretending not to notice but drawing herself ever so slightly more erect, the color rising in her cheeks, her breasts rising, not ostentatiously, her stomach flat in the harness of her ribs just below her diaphragm, where her music came from, and wires pulled, nerves and muscles pulled to the leg that sat athwart the other leg, displaying her brown skin with its bright down. He reached across to touch her knee. "Will you sing us something, Honey?"

"Oh, Babe," she said, drawing her knee away from him.

"Oh, would you, Cel?" Liz asked.

Boots knew she would. She loved to sing for them, though she needed to be coaxed a little. He said, "It's so lovely. The quiet and the dark and the candle. It's like a setting just for you." He touched her again, now on the arm. She was very brown, even in the shadows.

"But what shall I sing?"

"Sing 'Oro,' " Boots said.

She smiled and touched him back and nodded. She began to sing. When she did, Jenny turned, dropped her covered mason jar in the grass, and ran to her, throwing herself on Celia's knees. Seth and Jason stood still and silent. Boots sipped his gin and listened to the ancient air.

> I will hoist my sail for the west,
> Oro my little curragh, O.
> And I will not return until St. John's Eve,
> Oro my little boat.
> Oro my little curragh, O.
> Oro my little boat.

As she sang the old fisherman's song, Celia let her hand fondle Jenny's hair. She had sung it as a lullaby for years and had dandled Jenny at her knee to its melody. Jenny was the curragh—the boat—Celia sang in praise of.

Isn't my little boat beautiful floating in the harbor?
And the oars pulling strong and quietly.
How magnificently she leaps the high waves.
How light to carry up from the strand.

It delighted Farnham—though it did not surprise him anymore—that he, a shy, reserved man, should have fathered such a charmer as Jenny. He let his eyes fall to her from Celia. Though her hair was sun-bleached now and lighter than his, it was still red and he took great pleasure in recognizing it as his own hair, his mother's hair. What made Jenny precious to him was how she could, simply by being there, demolish his doubt about himself. Her slightest gesture or glance was enough to draw all his attention and hold it. It was not that she made requests of him, but that she was one, a constant appeal, more, an expectation. Jenny assumed that her father was in the world for her and the innocence with which she manifested her certainty of that made it so. He watched her at Celia's legs, her chin hooked over Celia's knee, her head moving slightly under Celia's hand. Farnham closed his own hand and opened it, remembering what touching his child felt like. Celia's song lulled him so that his looking at Jenny was neither conscious nor unconscious, but between. His mind was on his hand and its feeling of touching his child's red head, and then on the Irish fisherman's little boat, then on a dream of Jenny standing on a cliff at Mount Desert in Maine with the pink fluff of her nightgown blown by the wind, the fierce Atlantic wind that feathered her red hair and made her beautiful, a woman-child, regal, the world for her, all of it. Boots Farnham wanted everything for his girl.

He opened his hand and closed it, delighted, though not surprised, that he could feel Jenny's head without touching it. He sipped his warm gin and looked at Dick, big, red-faced friend, eyes bright behind steel-rimmed spectacles, a striped blue-and-white sailor's shirt, a massive chest, arms like tree limbs, at six feet three the biggest man Boots knew well. Yet Boots sat there thinking how like him he was. Dick was a plumber. He had gone a year to B.C. and then quit, but he was intelligent, sharp-witted, and kind. He was clumsy except when working, and then he was only strong and agile. But there was a bashfulness about him that was familiar to Boots, a bashfulness he understood. Dick stuttered occasionally, although never with Boots and Celia, who knew enough to take that as the best sign of their friendship.

Celia's song was over. Liz said, "Thank you, Cel," so softly that the mood did not fade. Jenny remained at Celia's knee. Seth and Jason were sitting in the grass, their mason jars before them blinking like neon, the fireflies.

Slowly there came the voices they needed to say good night to each other. They were seeing each other Monday, the adults; they had reserved bleachers tickets at Fenway for the Yankee game. Boston was leading by ten, but their hearts had been broken by the Sox before; Boots and Dick agreed that New York could still catch them.

The Dunns went off feeling already a pleasant anticipation of the next time, leaving Boots and Celia warm in the knowledge that their love included other loves.

Jenny said to Celia, "Mommy, let me," and then she leaned over and blew out the fat red candle on the wicker table. Celia said, "Take it into the house for me, Sweetie, and careful of the wax."

Boots wanted to stop Jenny from touching the candle. He was always more nervous than Celia about such things. They had fought about it and he knew that Celia was more right than he. Their little girl had to be led continually and gently into new, ever larger responsibilities. But candles made him nervous. Fire made him nervous. He watched her lift the doused candle slowly. She eyed it as if it were a sacred vessel and she carried it across the grass, up the three stairs and into the kitchen.

Celia stopped Boots from following her. "Wait, Babe, I want something from you."

"What?" Boots said. He wanted to make sure Jenny didn't light the thing again.

Celia put her arms around him. She said, "I've been falling all night. I want you to catch me."

He kissed and held her, pressed his cheekbone down into her shoulder. He saw with one eye Jenny's mason jar of fireflies lying in the grass, glowing still, but dimly. Perhaps the fireflies were suffocating each other? Boots wondered what made their tails light up, and did they burn when they rubbed each other like that?

"Don't you just love Dick and Liz?" Celia asked. "Don't you just love me?"

"I love everybody," Boots said. "But especially you." He could feel himself relaxing. His dull, inarticulate uneasiness faded. It was completely dark then. The fireflies encircled them, flitting on and off, and the other creatures' buzzing seemed louder. Celia and Boots stood holding each other, taking in the contours of each other's body, both so familiar, both so wonderfully new, as their bodies always were when they understood they were going to make love.

But then the cry. Jenny called from inside, called urgently.

Boots started to turn toward the door and felt a rush of fear. The yard with its square of rough lawn and its nylon-and-aluminum furniture and the downhanging locust tree against the barn, Boots's shop, was flooded with her cry. Nylon. Nylon melts. What was the nightgown made of? Nylon melts and becomes like napalm. Boots saw the form of his daughter approaching the door from inside. She was running, lit from behind, a silhouette. It was impossible to see her face, what was wrong. Her nightgown flew around her, but, backlit as she was, he saw her legs, her trunk. She could have been naked.

Perhaps that was why he stopped seeing her as Jenny. Suddenly, coming at him desperately, mouth agape in a screeching agony, was some other girl. Boots could feel his heart turning away, wanting not to know, a premonition; how he would turn forever from this memory, as he had turned from it before, even as his mind leapt to what it recognized—that naked Vietnamese girl running down the road, fleeing blindly, running at her photographer with fresh napalm bubbling her skin the way the sun in August bubbles tar. Boots remembered reading that such photographers put Vicks VapoRub in their nostrils to keep from smelling the scorched flesh they took pictures of.

"My fireflies!" Jenny cried, lurching down the steps and making for the jar in the grass.

"Relax, Sweetie," Celia said, laughing, turning toward the girl.

But Boots stopped her. "Hold me, Cel," he said. "*Me!*"

View of Jamaica Pond, Olmsted Park, 1894. BOSTON PUBLIC LIBRARY

State Street, 1930. Photograph by Berenice Abbott. BOSTON ATHENAEUM

Wooden houses on Linden Street, South Boston, 1930. Photograph by Walker Evans. BOSTON ATHENAEUM

Roxbury flood, February 1886. Photograph by Baldwin Coolidge. SOCIETY FOR THE PRESERVATION OF NEW ENGLAND ANTIQUITIES

West Church on Cambridge Street, West End. Photograph by Josiah Johnson Hawes. BOSTON ATHENAEUM

Boston City Hospital, opened in 1865. Photograph by Josiah Johnson Hawes, ca. 1865. BOSTON ATHENAEUM

The Doctors' City

My father was third and last in the line of Dr. Joseph Garlands. His host of patients in the Boston area called him Doctor Joe, and he drew bunny rabbits with his fountain pen on the thumbnails of children for taking their shots without a whimper . . . thumbs not sucked again until the ink wore off.

After the Second War Doctor Joe retired from the practice of pediatrics to run *The New England Journal of Medicine*, which under his editorship was read and reread from Chicago to Calcutta. For a while he was secretary of the Massachusetts Medical Society. Boston and Tufts universities awarded him honorary degrees on behalf of their medical schools, and he was elected an honorary fellow of the Royal Society of Medicine in England.

At the 150th anniversary in 1961 of his alma mater, the Massachusetts General Hospital, Pa's peers acclaimed him as one of its outstanding living graduates. When he retired from the *Journal* five years later, he resumed the part-time editorship of the *Harvard Medical School Alumni Bulletin*, which he had founded fifty years earlier, and was elected president of the Boston Medical Library.

So my father had his roots in every important sector of the Boston medical establishment.

Doctor Joe and Mira Crowell fell in love toward the end of the First War. She was a real beauty, one of the head nurses at the Mass. General, where she had trained and where he was a medical house officer, or "house pupil," in the M.G.H. parlance. The New Hampshire girl committed her next fifty-four years to extending and enhancing the useful life of a husband born with a permanently leaking heart, *patent ductus arteriosus*, and bedeviled by stomach ulcers.

My mother nursed my father through his final illness in 1973, day and night, so that he could make eighty, see his memoirs published, and die in his own bed. Her life mission completed, her husband gone forever, she suddenly failed. Her sense of balance went askew; she fell one day raking leaves, broke her hip, her course ran rapidly downhill physically and mentally, and she landed back in her beloved old M.G.H. Brain surgery briefly seemed to clear her head, but her depression was incurable and defied diagnosis. One day she was wheeled into the Ether Dome, the amphitheater where she had attended lectures as a student nurse, now the subject of the week on neurological grand rounds.

Finally, disoriented and weeping and terribly ill, Ma was sent home, as baffling a case as ever. The world's greatest hospital could do no more for her. Nine months after her husband, she died. Not until autopsy was the suspicion of inoperable brain tumor confirmed. And then, irony of ironies, her doctors wrote her up in cold and clinical detail—none was spared, not even the microphotographs of her diseased brain—for the renowned "Case Records of the Massachusetts General Hospital" in her late husband's medical journal.

That poignant, sudden denouement of love and life was in the family tradition. They would have wanted it that way, I am convinced. My father's striking survival into old age with a cardiac defect (today it is repairable) had already been recorded in the medical annals by his cardiologist and old friend Paul Dudley White. The course of my mother's case was in that same spirit—much harder to take, but nevertheless a dramatic illustration of the way the future of knowledge germinates in the humus of the past.

Here, wrapped up from presentation of case to anatomical diagnoses in *The New England Journal of Medicine*, was Ma's contribution to medical progress in the three classic areas of care, teaching, and research. A posthumous collaboration, you might say. And *Boston*, it strikes me, to the core.

You see, there really was nowhere else for Mira Garland to go. Medically, she was *there*, always had been, like Boston women who in the old days never bought hats because they already *had* them.

I have always heard that Boston medicine, even outside of Boston, is considered among the best in the world, perhaps the best. Chauvinism. How do you weigh such a claim, or assessment, short of a medical major-league playoff with a box score of urological hits, runs, and errors . . . and waiting-room post-mortem? As a layman I am not qualified to make an unprejudiced judgment about Boston's standing in the world of medicine. But perhaps my family involvement entitles me to make a stab at sketching the genesis of what today is too complex to describe except in the most general terms, and to separate out some of the roots that individually may not seem unique but that together have something to do with the great spread of the tree.

To begin with, the less said about the confusion of ignorance and quackery that passed for medical practice in Britain's American colonies the kinder, except that it was least harmful in such oases of enlightenment and fraternal feeling as Boston and Philadelphia. James Lloyd was an example of colonial enlightenment, a Bostonian who studied with the most skillful surgeons in England, returned home well trained, and transplanted through his practice and teaching the best principles then current in Europe.

The brightest of Dr. Lloyd's apprentices in Boston was young Joseph Warren, Harvard graduate and electrifying Revolutionary leader, who in his turn passed the torch of medical learning to his even younger brother John before expiring in a bloody blaze of wasted glory on Bunker Hill with a British bullet in his skull. John Warren served General Washington with such distinction in the Revolution and established such a reputation as a lecturer on anatomy and surgery in Boston after the war that Harvard College asked him in 1782 (the year after he had helped organize the Massachusetts Medical Society) to create its medical school and be the first professor.

If anything, Dr. John's son, John Collins Warren, was an even finer surgeon, with just as broad a view of their profession. In 1805 he and physician James Jackson took the lead in founding the Boston Medical Library, and in 1812 they produced the first issue of *The New England Journal of Medicine and Surgery*. Piece by piece the basis of Boston medicine was being put together, its foundation concretely laid in 1811 when Warren and Jackson persuaded the Brahmin establishment, with its Puritan conscience, to build the town's first bona fide hospital—even though admission of patients to the Massachusetts General Hospital was delayed ten years by the decision of the trustees to give priority to an insane asylum in Charlestown, the McLean Hospital (later removed to Belmont), one of the first in America to concentrate on the treatment (as opposed to the mere custodial care) of the mentally ill.

GARLAND *The Doctors' City*   125

Under the best of conditions, hospitals in those days bred and spread as much disease as they cured, and the place to be sick was at home, if you were lucky enough to have one. In founding the Mass. General, Warren and Jackson were motivated by a desire to care for the sick poor of Boston; but in addition they saw the need, then as now, for "teaching material" for the Harvard Medical School: in exchange for their privacy, hundreds of patients were brought under one roof for treatment.

Thus sprang up the historic partnership between the Harvard Medical School and the Massachusetts General Hospital, with their tradition of joint faculty and staff appointments based, as my father once wrote, "like the government of England, on certain unwritten conventions. By a tacit gentlemen's agreement both parties recognize their interdependence, and the representatives of both parties being gentlemen (frequently the same gentlemen!), mutual good will usually prevails."

At a time when Boston was commencing to take itself ever so seriously as the Athens of America, if not the world, it was a lucky thing all around that thousands of immigrants were arriving on these shores to turn (more than any water power) the wheels of the Industrial Revolution in New England, and some of the aged-in-the-vessels blood hereabouts from blue to red.

First the Boston City and then a spate of other hospitals, and the medical schools of Boston University (the old New England Female Medical College, first of its kind in the country) and Tufts College, were founded in response to the waves of new citizens, the public-health consciousness awakened by the Civil War, the sudden need for doctors, the dawning of the scientific revolution in medicine.

As the last century wound down, the structure of the medical center serving a spreading metropolitan area rose upon the Harvard-M.G.H. foundation. Today the affiliations through the three medical schools—joined by a new fourth one at the University of Massachusetts—interconnect bewilderingly with the Massachusetts Institute of Technology, scores of hospitals, health and research institutions, journals, clubs, and societies, regionally, nationally, worldwide, in a web of communication and service that would stagger, as it frequently does, the hardiest computer.

The world's rarest, toughest, most unyielding cases, princes and paupers, have found their way like pilgrims to Boston, to recover, to benefit, to live if they can, by what Boston in its wisdom has to offer, and to add their own abrasive histories to the continuous, mind-whetting diagnostic-therapeutic process that goes on here night and day. As our doctors have attracted patients from near and far, the patients and their doctors have magnetized to Boston students who then root here to enrich the medical soil or else carry their handful of it back to the corners of the earth whence they came. Suffice it that Harvard is the Western world's most prolific source of medical-school professors.

Beside that incredibly computerized fount of knowledge, the Countway Library of Medicine at Harvard Medical School, there grows a plane tree cut from the original on the Mediterranean island of Cos under which Hippocrates is said to have lectured his disciples, a patient frequently on hand, no doubt, for demonstration. So it is that in Boston today, if you can put up with the bedside parades of preceptors and pupils, and the patting and poking and pricking and prodding, you can rest assured (if not easy) that whatever ails you, you're at the point of the action, on the frontier of medical knowledge.

What has been the part played in all this eminence by that amorphous element of institutional genetics called tradition? It is heavy but not overpowering to the strong personality. In 1846, twenty-five years almost to the day after the opening of his hospital, Dr. John Collins Warren removed a tumor from the jaw of a patient in the first public demonstration in history of surgery under ether. The patient awoke and mumbled that he had felt no pain. "Gentlemen, this is no humbug," Dr. Warren announced brusquely to his amazed colleagues, and Dr. Oliver Wendell Holmes dubbed the miracle *anesthesia*— Dr. Holmes, Boston's literary terrier, Harvard's anatomist who was the first to describe the route by which doctors unconsciously transmitted childbed fever from mother to mother.

That is how the Ether Dome in the M.G.H.'s classically compact nucleus, the Bulfinch Building, got its name ... the same amphitheater where my great-grandfather and his son and his grandson attended their lectures, and where my mother had been learner and, more than half a century later, lesson. At this hospital the founder's son, J. Mason Warren, introduced plastic surgery to America, and to the M.G.H. his grandson, J. Collins Warren, brought from Scotland the techniques of asepsis, making modern surgery possible;

young Warren returned from the same wards of Dr. Joseph Lister in Glasgow where my grandfather followed the great man in his rounds during *his* European tour of study.

And then there was Zabdiel Boylston, way back, conqueror of smallpox in America, . . . and other old Boston names, the Shattucks, Mixters, Bigelows, Richardsons . . . and newer ones—Reginald Fitz, first to recognize appendicitis; Walter Cannon, giant among modern physiologists; his sister Ida and Richard Cabot, pioneers in medical social service; fiery Harvey Cushing of the Peter Bent Brigham Hospital, keenest of brain surgeons; George Minot, William Murphy, and George Whipple at Boston City Hospital, who shared the Nobel Prize for discovering the treatment of pernicious anemia . . . and Elliott Joslin of the New England Deaconess Hospital, who kept the diabetic Dr. Minot alive to complete *his* work; Fritz Lipmann, whose explorations of intermediary metabolism won him a Nobel Prize, John Enders, Thomas Weller, and Frederick Robbins at the Children's Medical Center, Nobel laureates in the victory over poliomyelitis . . .

Where to begin, where to stop? The roster of the greats of Boston medicine would populate another frieze around the Public Library, with names to spare.

Tradition is deep in the Boston scene—thank God for it (and the Cabots and the Lodges, too)—and your true Bostonian knows the difference between reverence and respect. Fifty-five years ago my father (whom I began by revering and ended by respecting) came across a battered old desk at the M.G.H. at which his fellow house pupils had written their case reports and on which they had scratched their signatures—scores of them, including his father's, his uncle's, and his own—at least back to 1851. Editorializing about his find, he wrote: "In our worship of the Brand New we have scant time for a fitting veneration of that which has gone before and proven its worth and left its mute reminders; not that we have no antiquarians among us; not but that many of us respect the accomplishments that laid the foundations for our own successes, but by and large we are too engrossed in the strivings of the present to pay more than a passing respect to the labor of those who have achieved success before us, and to the methods by which they achieved it."

Scant time for veneration, indeed. Many years later Dr. Edward D. Churchill, chief of surgery at the Mass. General, stumbled on the autographed house-pupils' desk in a service area behind the hospital, on its way to the dump. Today it is safely ensconced in the M.G.H. museum. How fitting that this banged-up Hippocratean artifact from the archaeological core of Boston medicine, so absentmindedly discarded by the proprietors of the present, should have been rescued for the keepers of the future by a small-town Illinois boy drawn to the mecca, enriching immeasurably its medicine—and, as one of the very distinguished surgeons of his generation, its traditions!

That same quality of flexibility, of limberness, that characterizes a vigorous old age in the institution as in the man—respect for the form of the heritage without reverence for the substance—inspired the trustees of the Massachusetts General Hospital to take the startlingly bold step a few years ago of raising from the middle ranks to the directorship the late John Knowles, a brilliantly versatile young physician who enjoyed telling how he had been denied admission to the Harvard Medical School because he was not of a sufficiently serious nature, the word of his capers at college having preceded him (a wonderful instance of institutional self-perpetuation, as long since elevated to an art in Boston).

What of the present, and the future? The problems universally associated with modern health service—rocketing costs and creeping impersonality—are nowhere more evident, and, fortunately, talked about, than in a great world medical center such as Boston, which has a corner on neither economic wisdom nor tender loving care.

Of social conscience, the Puritan ethic, or just warm steam from the melting pot, however, we seem to have as goodly a supply as ever. Governor John Winthrop settled Boston in 1630 and also doctored his constituents with "Help for our Bodies by Physick." Three hundred and fifty years passed, and the senior United States Senator from Massachusetts was doctoring on a grander scale under the banner of national health insurance.

As for the tender heart, how can the well treat the ill other than with compassion, however much machinery intervenes? A hundred years ago my great-grandfather slogged through three-foot snowdrifts, carrying his nurse in his arms, to a patient's door. My grandfather would never refuse a house call and was driven to an early grave by the demands of his practice and his conscience.

Many a sound sleep was broken by the midnight telephone call and the rumble of my father's car starting up. When her nurses at her old hospital were told that my mother had at last died at home, they wept.

"When in distress, every man becomes our neighbor," importuned James Jackson and John Collins Warren in their letter a hundred and seventy years ago urging the establishment in Boston of a general hospital, "one which would afford relief and comfort to thousands of the sick and miserable."

Adherence to that admonition of compassion has been the distinguishing mark of Boston medicine to this day, and there is no reason to suppose that it will not be as strongly, if not so simply, the guiding principle of the future.

Frontispiece of the pamphlet "Stop Thief, or King Calomel Outlawed," published pseudonymously by the Hon. Fredrick Fact, 1834. FRANCIS A. COUNTWAY LIBRARY

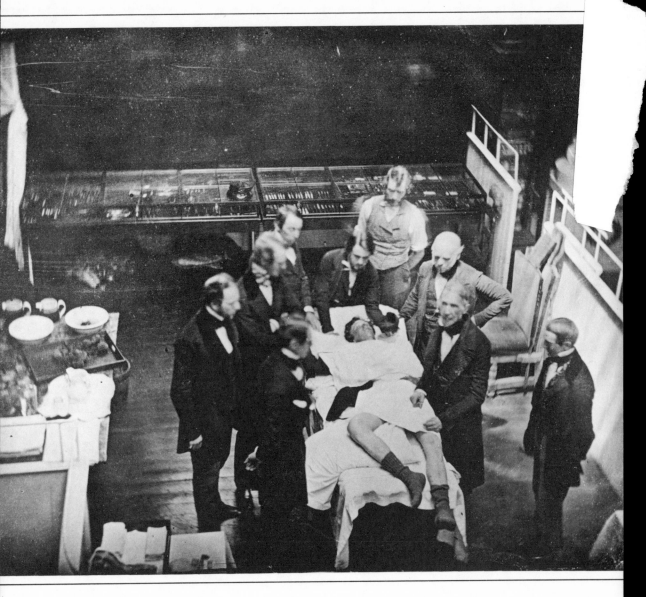

One of the earliest ether operations, on a woman at the Massachusetts General Hospital. This photograph (ca. 1903) was made from a daguerreotype taken in the Ether Dome by Josiah Johnson Hawes, 1847. MASSACHUSETTS GENERAL HOSPITAL

"Boston, from the S. East," mid-19th century lithograph by Jenkins & Colburn.
BOSTON ATHENAEUM

View of Boston Harbor from Atlantic Avenue, ca. 1880. BOSTON PUBLIC LIBRARY

Logan Airport, October 29, 1928. AERIAL PHOTOS OF NEW ENGLAND, INC., NORWOOD

The Battle of Maverick Street

In the mid-1960s East Boston seemed—like some tiny Balkan nation ringed by land-hungry neighbors fairly salivating at the prospect of a choice morsel— on the verge of disappearing. Physically, "Eastie" was shrinking at an alarming rate. The barons of nearby Logan International Airport looked into East Boston's future and saw long stretches of runway where freshly done wash, hung from back-porch clotheslines, now flapped in the breeze. The czars of the turnpike authority gazed at Eastie and saw a third harbor tunnel; to them, East Boston was a Polish Corridor, useful for the army of trucks and cars that moved daily in and out of the city. Not to be outdone, the rulers of the Department of Public Works envisioned a new, broad highway between Eastie and neighboring Winthrop. The signs seemed to indicate that in very little time East Boston would become an urban Atlantis, and its brand of civilization, ethnic American, would be remembered only in song and legend. Its people would scatter and its new inhabitants would be hangars, warehouses, oil tanks, and containerization facilities.

It would have been a shoddy end for a proud community, one that had served as the gateway to Boston since the 1800s, when it was known as Noddle Island. It was the port of debarkation for generations of immigrants, first the Nova Scotians and the Irish, the latter fleeing their lovely but riven isle. Patrick Kennedy, grandfather of JFK, owned a tavern in the area and practiced the arts of ward politics, skills that were not exactly abandoned by his descendants. The Irish were followed by the sons and daughters of Abruzzi and Calabria, who, by their numbers, gave East Boston a distinctly Mediterranean flavor by the mid-twentieth century. But Eastie's geographic location— by the sea, by the airport—made it a prime victim in the age of the jet plane and the automobile. People flying off to vacation in the Virgins cared little for the streets with their neat rows of wooden houses that had been home for a family for three generations. Impatient commuters cursed as they sat snarled in traffic at the tunnel entrance; so what if another few hundred homes had to disappear if another tunnel could crawl across the bottom of the harbor? They wanted a quick way to get to work and then back to their half acre of nature in a tract development probably named for Paul Revere.

Eastie's future looked bleak a little more than a decade ago. But today, with Boston nearing its fourth century, East Boston has not vanished. It is a vital urban neighborhood, displaying a level of both citizen action and political savvy out of proportion to its size. True, the shuddering hulks of the big jets still shake the lamps in living rooms and obliterate conversation at times, but the airport is not the leviathan it once was. Certainly one could not say it has been tamed—but at least it has been held at bay, made more tractable.

The rampaging bureaucracy, its head dizzy with visions of ramps and tunnels and warehouses and oil tanks, has been slowed. It is safe to say that a revolution occurred in East Boston, not an untypical event for this particular city. It began, however, in a very unlikely place, in a small courtyard tucked away on an urban street in the shadow of the lowering jets, and it was begun by a group of people who bore scant resemblance to the guys who threw the tea in the harbor. In fact, they weren't "guys" at all, they were women, and hardly the sort one would expect to go about fomenting rebellion. They were mothers and grandmothers, the kind you think of baking cookies and lasagne and asking for funds for the PTA. These particular women did those things, but threw in a little extracurricular activity—you can call it civil disobedience, or street action, or protest—or you can call it revolution. Some people today remember it as "The Battle of Maverick Street."

It was October of 1968 and the women of Maverick Street were angry. They had a right to be. For not only was Maverick Street jammed cheek by jowl with the airport and its noise factory, but it was also being used as a thoroughfare for trucks carrying fill—dirt, to be exact—for the building of another runway area. And, to add insult to injury, the filling of Bird Island flats was being done illegally, without the required permit.

On many days, more than six hundred trucks rumbled down Maverick Street, not only creating constant noise but forcing the mothers to forbid their children to play on the sidewalks. Mothers also wondered what the stench of gasoline and the exhaust fumes were doing to their children's lungs, not to mention to the paint jobs on the houses.

For Maverick Street was not just an indifferent city thoroughfare. A walk along its length would dispel that notion. The houses, mainly the three-story wood structures that one finds throughout Boston, bore the touches of the proud, live-in owner, not the neglect of the absentee landlord. One house might be painted a sparkling Mediterranean pink; another might sport a new facade, lovingly placed over the old timbers, of rough textured stone or brick; in the window of another home one could see, fluttering in the breeze, the delicate traceries of lace. Flower boxes bloomed on windowsills and private homes coexisted with small businesses—sub shops, ma-and-pa grocery stores.

At first the women in the area grumbled at home, then they started to talk to one another, and then they began to meet, often in the home of Anna De Fronzo on Lamson Court. Mrs. De Fronzo was in her sixties then, a widow, grandmother of fifteen, a woman with an expressive face that brings to mind the face of another Anna—Magnani, the great Italian film actress. Anna De Fronzo served homemade cake and talked of revolt.

"This is where it all started," she said years later, gesturing at the small courtyard around her. "The four or five years that we were begging the Port Authority to keep the trucks off of Maverick Street we were having little meetings, maybe ten women, and we weren't getting any satisfaction. So one evening we had a meeting in here and we decided this was it, and that someday I would give them a call and we would get out in the streets. It happened on a Saturday morning and it was really bad. They were filling in Bird Island flats illegally and that was our cue to start going out on the streets, and every night this is where we met, in this alley, this is where we had our coffee, and where we decided what we were going to do the next day."

On that October Saturday the Maverick Street women took what can best be described as direct action in the tradition of the Sons of Liberty. They went out into the street wearing their housedresses, some clutching their children by the hand, and blocked the road with their bodies. The trucks could not pass. Mayor Kevin White responded by banning heavy truck traffic on Maverick Street.

But then the Port Authority counterattacked. It sought, and got, a court injunction against the city's ban on trucks. The battle had been joined; the whites of the eyes exposed. The women, jubilant at the news of the city ban, were furious at the injunction. Anna De Fronzo said angrily, "Headlines this morning, we win. Headlines this evening, we lost. I don't give a damn. Let them arrest me. People have taken too much. They're fed up to here. Wait, they tell us, wait. So we wait for years and nothing happens!"

The women of Maverick Street were not about to withdraw from the field of battle. At first, the men were reluctant to join them.

"It was the women," remembers Anna. "All women. Maybe there would be one or two men who would come and listen and give us advice, but when it came to going out into the streets, I think the men in East Boston weren't so brave. They didn't want to get arrested. They didn't want to get picked up by the police. They were afraid of going to court."

The men, Anna said, seemed to accept a defeat they saw as inevitable. "The women would come right out and fight. That was what happened on Maverick Street. It was only women when the police came—but when the men saw we were being abused by the state police, then they got into it."

On a Tuesday morning the women were ready; they had tasted success once, and it was sweet in their mouths. They had stopped the trucks, the city was on their side, and no one was going to take away a victory so hard won. So the women moved onto Maverick Street, about thirty women with children, marching in a circle. A truck pulled up and stopped. One of the women, Rosemarie Bottaro, shouted, "Three days of fighting. Three days of peace. You think we're gonna stop now?" Another woman called to a group of men standing across the street, "Come on, you guys. We're doing this for you, too!" They began to sing the anthem of the civil-rights movement, "We Shall Overcome."

A policeman walked up to the women and said he had a court order to clear the streets. The women and children sat down on the streets and the police had to drag them away. Anna wound up black and blue; a nine-year-old girl got bruise marks on her neck and arms when she was hauled from the street.

The women regrouped in Lamson Court. They had an ally in Fred Salvucci, the manager of the Little City Hall in Eastie, and in Kevin White, who surveyed the scene and announced that despite the injunction he would enforce the ban on trucks, because, in this volatile situation, they were a danger to public safety.

The negotiations dragged on for a few days, but in the end, the Port Authority capitulated. The trucks would use a private road on Port Authority property, and would steer clear of Maverick Street. The women had won. The Battle of Maverick Street was over, and it was the irregulars who carried the day.

In East Boston this was the beginning of an activist period that continues to the present. The citizens would not win every battle. Not long after Maverick Street, they marched again to try to save Amerena Field, a large tract of open space; despite their efforts, the field became a post office. But the important thing was that they had learned they *could* win—a lesson that was being learned in other Boston neighborhoods, as well. As one of the women said, "We had a defeatist attitude before. We used to say, 'They're so big you can't beat them.' Now people feel they can beat them!"

Anna said, "This has taught us a lesson. You just can't sit around and talk with people. They don't listen to you. You have to go out to the streets. That's the only way they will listen to you."

For Anna De Fronzo, Maverick Street was the beginning of her career as a community activist. She is now in her seventies, and has become an extremely skillful political operative. She still has all the warmth and good humor of the Italian grandmother she looks like—and is—but in the same breath that she mentions her grandchildren she can toss around words like "fiscal autonomy" and "eminent domain." She can complain about a state official that he promised her something "on the air" when they shared a TV panel show, but he hasn't delivered yet.

Anna is certainly not your average neighborhood woman, but neither is she one of a kind. For in Boston's neighborhoods a new breed of leader has emerged, and this breed is urban, female, and unafraid of "authority." These women belie the stereotype of what the sociologists call the "Working-Class Woman," who is often described as passive, home-oriented, unwilling to venture outside the world of home and family.

In fact, for many of Boston's urban activists, their public roles did begin when they became involved in issues that hit close to home and family. Anna, for example, started collecting for such charities as the March of Dimes, and this volunteer effort enabled her to come to know many East Boston women, making her a natural leader in the Maverick Street crisis. The women went into the streets with her, she says, "Because they love East Boston, they have their children here, they love their homes, they don't want to lose them. Every time I see them in the Liberty Market they say, 'Call me, Anna, if you need me.' I've got women interested who never got out of the house before."

In many of Boston's neighborhoods the men work long hours at physically demanding jobs, and it is the women who find themselves dealing with local issues—the dangerous corner that doesn't have a stoplight, the chemical trucks routed down a residential street, the park about to be gobbled up by some institution. At first, the women may be awed by the three-piece suits of the lawyers, the jargon of the bureaucrats, the professional charm of the corporate representatives. But they see themselves as being in a battle for their homes and their children, for their own "turf," and so they hang tough. And then they discover an interesting fact—that they are intelligent, "street smart," and that they, too, can learn the jargon. They start to get involved in other issues. After Maverick Street, Anna wanted to find a site for housing for the elderly, and with the help of Fred Salvucci she located a prime spot. She said to some of the elderly residents of Eastie, "You take your chairs and just sit down on that spot and don't let them build anything else there." They said to her, "You get the chairs and we'll be there!"

Anna says, "Some people think I'm a rabble-rouser, but I don't think so. If you don't go out and fight, nobody listens."

But in fact, the street confrontations are rare. Most of Anna's work is done in long hours of meetings (one week she had 23 meetings), in which complex issues such as zoning laws and government regulations are dealt with. Like many of Boston's urban activists, she has become well versed in the language of the law. "If I knew then what I know now, the airport would never have got Wood Island," she says. Wood Island was a large and spacious park that the airport plowed under for runways in the 1950s. "It was our fault for letting them grab it."

In many cases, neighborhood women feel freer than men to press hard on community issues, because, unlike men, they are not as vulnerable to economic pressures. Often they have no paid job from which to be fired, no promotion on the line; if they do work outside the home they are rarely in high-level positions that would be threatened by political activity. In addition, they get the kind of comfort and support from one another that helps to keep them going; the meetings in Lamson Court were important in keeping the Maverick Street effort on the track. For most of these women, their family lives continue to be of tremendous importance, and Lamson Court is very much like an extended family. In the summer, Anna awakens early, takes her newspaper and coffee out to the courtyard, and before long other neighbors are out, chatting. Anna's married daughter lives on the court and there are always grandchildren around. "Italian people are very strong in cousins, nieces, nephews," Anna says. "Children live near their parents—they're not in California or Florida. They stay here."

Anna says that in the nearly thirty years she has lived on the court she's never felt she had to lock her door or worry about anything left in the yard. On summer evenings all the neighbors have a barbecue in the courtyard and stay up late, talking long into the night. It is a style of life that is precious to a great many people, and it is no wonder they do not wish to see it disappear.

For many urban activists, their concerns remain focused on their home community, although they have learned that other communities have the same problems. Mary Ellen Welch, an East Boston activist and a colleague of Anna's, remembers the first time she saw Saundra Graham, a community leader from Cambridge, on television. It was just after Graham had led a group of Cambridge residents onto the podium at a Harvard graduation and seized the microphone from startled academics.

"She was talking," says Mary Ellen," and she reminded me of us. She said 'We're here to stay and no one's going to push us out!' They're fighting for housing over there, and Harvard is taking it. It could have been us, talking about the airport."

At times the neighborhood leaders reach out to people in other communities to work together on citywide issues. Some East Bostonians were surprised to see a car full of dashiki-clad blacks in one of their airport demonstrations; and both suburban and urban community activists joined in the successful fight to stop the Inner Belt, a highway proposed in the sixties that would have ripped through many of Boston's neighborhoods. Such joint efforts are difficult—the people involved are working on their own time, with no salary and no high-paid consultant help. But the networks that exist can come together for mutual aid in a time of need.

If East Boston's renaissance in the 1960s owed much to a cadre of devoted citizen-activists, it was also accelerated by some remarkable and dedicated city workers. "Public servants" are often thought of as flaccid bureaucrats, whose purpose seems to be to preserve the status quo and avoid making decisions. But the Little City Hall trailer in Maverick Square has been headquarters for a group of people who take the notion of public service very seriously. Kevin White set up the Little City Hall network across the city, and one of his happiest appointments was that of Fred Salvucci as manager of the East Boston unit. Salvucci had the ability to beat the technocrats at their own game when they started to pull out charts and graphs to illustrate why a new highway was absolutely necessary, or why the economy would collapse without another runway plunked down on what was now a row of houses. Fred has a degree in engineering from M.I.T.; but even more important, he has a gut-level understanding of the Italian-American urban culture. He was part of it in East Boston (and today he still lives, in Brighton, in a three-decker between relatives on the first and third floors). Because he can speak fluent Italian, he was able to explain to confused and frightened old people the complexities of moving into housing for the elderly. But more than anything it was Fred's commitment to the community that really made him an integral part of Eastie. One year he went away for a vacation in Maine and refused to give anyone his number, so he wouldn't be bothered—but then he came back to Eastie four times that week to make sure everything was running smoothly.

Mary Ellen Welch remembers one meeting where a number of city council members had come down to a hearing on an elderly-housing project for East Boston. Before the project could be built, the land had to be taken by eminent domain by the Boston Housing Authority. In the past, Boston neighborhoods had fought pitched battles with the BRA over land seizures, but in this case the community approved. The politicians launched into attacks on the BRA, which did not impress the savvy Eastie residents.

"The people in the audience from East Boston knew more about the steps involved in getting elderly housing than the politicians did," Mary Ellen says.

"These guys hadn't done their homework and all they were doing was trying to attack the BRA for its past sins. One of them started giving Freddie a hard time. He kept saying to Freddie, 'You haven't answered my question.' But Fred *had* answered his question. Well, we all started to mutter. Then finally, one woman said, 'O.K., everybody up!' and we all started yelling, 'Leave Freddy alone! Leave Freddy alone!' We protect our own."

East Boston is still at it today, protecting its own. It had always done so, in a private way, but the neighborhood learned how to act in a public way, as well, against outside forces that once seemed invincible. Eastie is no longer an endangered species, though the price of survival is constant vigilance. Its quality endures. Anna De Fronzo, speaking of her courtyard, might have been speaking for all of Eastie: "It's our little country, it's something different. Strangers come here and sit with us and they love it. Once they come, they always come back."

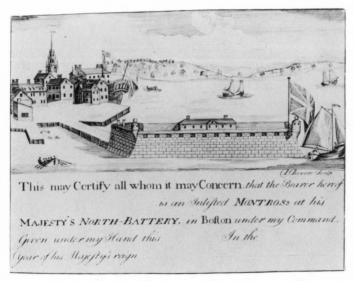

Enlistment certificate with a view of North Battery. Engraving by Paul Revere, ca. 1762. MASSACHUSETTS HISTORICAL SOCIETY

Minority Priority

Boston's very proud of its minorities,
  Delighted to be polyglot,
But according to the relevant authorities,
  A melting pot is what it's not.

Italian, Irish, Slavic and Hebraic now
  Are sedulously sticking to their own,
Which makes the Boston picture a mosaic now,
  With every group as solid as a stone.

The reason is the hard and fast conviction felt
  By the members of each ethnic group
That as soon as a minority begins to melt,
  It's bound to wind up in the soup.

Triple deckers in Dorchester, 1977. EUGENE RICHARDS

Corner of Pinckney and Joy Streets, 1930. Photograph by Berenice Abbott. BOSTON ATHENAEUM

146   A BOOK FOR BOSTON

Abraham Avery House (center), 44 Union Park, South End, ca. 1885. THE
BOSTONIAN SOCIETY

Abraham Avery house, second bedroom, ca. 1885. THE BOSTONIAN SOCIETY

Children's playroom, 3 Oakland Street, Roxbury, 1890. Photograph by Henry Hadcock. SOCIETY FOR THE PRESERVATION OF NEW ENGLAND ANTIQUITIES

John F. Fitzgerald ("Honey Fitz"), mayor of Boston 1906-07 and 1910-13, at an opening day Red Sox game. BOSTON PUBLIC LIBRARY

Childhood's Song

Baseball was religion for us. If the players were gods, the broadcasters were priests, linking us with Olympus through the magic of radio. On my father's big old cathedral-shaped Stromberg Carlson, we listened to Jim Britt tell of the Red Sox and the Braves, and on rainy days we heard him do telegraphic re-creations of out-of-town games from the studio, with no crowd noise, and the telegraph key chattering in the eerie quiet.

But it wasn't just Jim Britt we heard, and it wasn't just Boston teams. From New York we heard Mel Allen report the Yankee games, and Russ Hodges do the Giants, and Red Barber do the Dodgers. In fact my most vivid baseball memory is neither visual nor Bostonian. I remember Red Barber's soft, precise Floridian voice on opening day in 1947 when Jackie Robinson first took the field. "Robinson is definitely brunette," Barber said, and that image of black skin and white uniform and green grass, for the first time in conjunction at the start of a major-league spring, stays on as if I had seen it.

The announcers brought the parks alive, too, ball parks that in our imagination were the point and purpose of cities we'd never seen, cities that were created to provide fans for the ball games. Braves Field we knew, with the jury box in right and the railroad yards beyond left field, and the river beyond the yards. Fenway Park we still know: the Wall, the scoreboard (different board, same location), where Williams used to chat with the operators, the Cities Service sign in Kenmore Square. But they were not much more real than the places we imagined, the cities with the affectionate nicknames, the parks with their own peculiar landscape: Briggs Stadium in the Motor City with the pavilion in right; Forbes Field in the Smoky City, where Greenberg

Gardens was; Comisky Park in the Windy City, and Wrigley Field with the ivy on the walls; Shibe Park in the City of Brotherly Love; Crosley Field in the Rhineland. To this day when I see one of those places in my travels I am thrilled.

We did most of our listening to baseball after dark. During the day we played it ourselves, but at night we heard the voices drifting in, often from far away, and the crowd noise, and the bat sounds. It was so clear in our minds: the grass bright green under the lights, the gray road uniforms, the white home uniforms, the base paths red brown, the players moving. Ted Williams had a little knee dip we tried to imitate. Bob Elliot had a bat waggle we weren't strong enough to imitate.

We knew how everyone looked. We only had to see a player once. We knew the way DiMaggio stood, feet spread, bat nearly straight. We knew that Stan Musial looked like he was hitting around a corner. We knew that the ground baked hard in Sportsman's Park, so that the ball bounced higher and scooted faster. We knew that a ball pulled down either line at the Polo Grounds (in the shadow of Coogan's Bluff) was a short and easy homer. We knew that if Williams had played at Yankee Stadium and DiMaggio (the last name by itself always meant Joe—Dom was "The Little Professor" and Vince didn't count) had played at Fenway, both would have broken Ruth's record (which was considered unbreakable). We knew that the Red Sox were spoiled, a rich-kid's team. We knew the Braves were blue collar and honest. With the same prescience that Jim Britt showed, we backed the Braves. You could count on them.

In 1946 the Braves opened against the Dodgers. The Braves had people like 'Bama Rowell that year, and Johnny Hopp, and Dick Culler at shortstop. It was the year Carl Furillo broke in with the Dodgers. What lingers most in memory from that time is the still-wet paint on the reserved grandstand seats and the orderly green stripes across the backs of most of the fans as they trudged out, after the game, onto Gaffney Street.

The Red Sox won the pennant that year, and the Braves won a pennant two years later. Neither won the World Series, and no one won anything else for a very long time thereafter. But that only mattered at the time. It doesn't matter now. Now the names matter: Earl Torgeson, Phil Masi, Tommy

Holmes, Bobby Doerr, Vern Stephens, Stan Spence, Clint Conatser, Sibbi Sisti, Billy Hitchcock, Matt Batts. And names, too, of the loyal opposition: Ken Keltner, Red Schoendist, Cliff Mapes, Gene Hermanski, Pat Millin, Del Ennis.

The Braves went to Milwaukee before the 1953 season. Childhood's end. For fifty years it had been as fixed as the Ptolemaic universe: two leagues, sixteen teams in ten cities, none farther south than Washington, none farther west than St. Louis. Fifty years. Always. And then they were gone. We felt as Galileo must have as he looked up and muttered, "Still they move."

And the announcers came and went. Leo Egan followed Jim Britt. Curt Gowdy came down from New York after apprenticing with Mel Allen. Bob Delaney spoke to us, too, and Bob Murphy, Bill Crowley, Ken Coleman, Ned Martin, Jim Woods, Dick Stockton.

It was Martin and Woods who understood us best of all, who knew that baseball unified us, made us cosmopolitan. It wasn't merely Municipal Stadium in Cleveland, it was "the big ball park by the lake." It wasn't merely Yankee Stadium, it was "the big stadium in the Bronx." Ballplayers weren't just ballplayers, they were Texans and Michiganders. They had hometowns and middle names.

Woods localized the game and helped us keep that sense of village connectedness that had been born long ago in front of the cathedral-shaped radio as we sat at night listening to the familiar voices carrying across the dark fields of the Republic, recounting the changeless ritual. Ned Martin reminded us that baseball is a game of wit and intelligence. Woods kept alive our sense of wonder. Between them they were perfect. Only Red Barber was their equal. We shall not see their like again.

It was that sense of community and connection that baseball gave us all. The sense of participation with people in Cleveland and St. Louis and Detroit, joined in the same celebration; the sense of kinship with others in their cars on a late Sunday in August with the windows open, driving home slowly from the beach. The Red Sox lead the A's eleven-three in game two of a doubleheader. The crowd has thinned, there isn't much noise. The voices of the vendors are clear on the crowd mike. Dick Gernert is at first for Boston, Ferris Fain at bat for Philadelphia. Mel Parnell coasts in to an easy win over

PARKER *Childhood's Song*   153

Carl Scheib (Dick Fowler in the third, Charlie Bishop in the fifth). The Red Sox would finish sixth that year, the A's fourth. We listened not for the results but for the lulling sound of the game and the music of the names: Eddie Joost, Faye Throneberry, Elmer Valo, Al Zarilla.

Sometimes girl friends or wives or mothers or sisters, who knew no better (they were sexist times; there were things most women didn't understand), would ask the score, as if the score mattered. They could never understand why we listened and didn't know the score. They didn't understand that it was pattern, that it was the song of childhood we listened to, the romance of summer.

The hero of romance is always our superior, though he, too, is finally time's captive: John Sain, Warren Spahn, Tommy Holmes from the departed Braves; Ted Williams alone among the Red Sox, perhaps alone among Boston athletes. Ted Williams. The only man in fifty years to hit .400. The only man in forty-four years to hit .388. The ultimate hitter. He belongs in Boston's special place, where Bob Cousy and Bill Russell and Bobby Orr endure. And yet . . . Carl Michael Yastrzemski.

For me, Yaz is a perfect embodiment of the city and of the game he has played here so long. Williams, like Cousy, like Russell, like Bobby Orr, came nearly untarnished from the hand of God, so intuitive, so graceful, so well wrought that what he did is barely credible in ordinary terms. But Yaz . . . Yaz was forged in the crucible of will. Like the people who founded the city in which he has played out his adult life, Yaz is a tribute to industry and effort. He is self-made.

In 1966 Yaz batted .278, hit 16 home runs, and drove in 80. That winter he went to a health club in Lynnfield and worked on strength and flexibility. In 1967 he batted .326, hit 44 home runs, drove in 126. The Triple Crown. A re-creation.

But the numbers alone don't speak of 1967. They merely hint. No athlete in my memory has had such a year in so many ways. It is hard to imagine one that could exceed it. What was necessary Yaz produced. In the final two games of the season, with the pennant at stake, he went six for eight. Incredible.

Here is the American dream, the one that populated the sleep of all those durable Separatists who incorporated this old town 350 years ago. The dream assumed the possibility of self-creation through hard work and an unremitting exercise of will. Yaz is a visible expression of that dream. Forty years of age at this writing, but with a new stance, Yaz continues as he always has done, carrying in his person the collective aspirations of our city. He is, I think, heroic. When his virtues come to seem old-fashioned—only then will Boston itself grow old.

Carl Yastrzemski ("Yaz"), 1979.
THE BOSTON RED SOX

Garden Variety

The two Boston Gardens are poles apart:
    One offers the swanboat and duck
While the other appeals to the sport fan's heart
    As the home of the hoop and the puck.

The one that's called Public's entirely free,
    The other is anything but,
Which stops neither basketball devotee
    Nor passionate hockey nut.

One Garden's a glorious sylvan retreat,
    As verdant as all out-of-doors,
The other lets no grass grow under the feet
    But rejoices in parquetted floors.

A stranger in town on a sightseeing tour,
    Who has taken it into his head
To visit The Garden had better make sure
    Down which Garden path he'll be led.

The Pittsburgh Pirates vs. the Boston Americans (later the Red Sox), at the Huntington Avenue ballpark, World Series game, October 3, 1903. BOSTON PUBLIC LIBRARY, PRINT DEPARTMENT, MCGREEVY COLLECTION

JOHN KENNETH GALBRAITH

The Quite Elegant Future of Boston

In contemplating the future of Boston, I take as a metaphor, more accurately perhaps as a paradigm, the investments of Harvard University. Over the last century or more, Harvard has amassed a very substantial financial endowment. This is invested in stocks and bonds and some real estate, and the management of this largesse has always been the responsibility of the finest Boston financial minds. I think it fair to say that no resource of State Street—intellectual, social, mathematical, or intuitive—has been absent from this responsibility and this effort.

Harvard, though for a shorter time, has had another estate. That is in art. This has been under the management of the financially deviant offspring of the great financial families or professors concerned with the subject. These have included Edward Forbes of an old Boston merchant family, Paul Sachs of the great Wall Street house of Goldman Sachs, and, in more recent times, John Coolidge of, needless to say, the Coolidges. It would be going much too far—though for purposes of dramatization I've often gone that far—to say that these other sons and their colleagues and successors were men (and one woman) who would not be trusted with their own checkbooks. They would, indeed, be so trusted. But none was ever thought of as sharing the financial genius of the men who ran the financial endowment. They would never have dreamed of so regarding themselves.

The lesson to which I now come is this: The investments in the Harvard art estate in recent times have appreciated at a rate many times that of the stocks and bonds. By some calculations, although no precise calculation is possible, the value of the university's artistic estate now approaches that of

OPPOSITE: *Southwest corner of the Isabella Stewart Gardner Museum,* 1902. ISABELLA STEWART GARDNER MUSEUM

159

its financial endowment. Wise aesthetic investment has far outstripped financial genius. So, in appraising the future of Boston, as in assessing its past, it is the beginning of wisdom to mistrust the practical men. They are worthy and self-confident. But they have been wrong in the past, and we can reasonably suggest, even if our instinct is of the most compassionate sort, that they will be wrong in the future. They will not see what is most important—even by somber economic calculation.

Forty-odd years ago, when I first came to Boston, there was no doubt as to the explanations, expectations, and recommendations of the practical men for the future. Boston was the pivot of the manufacturing industries of New England. These were cotton textiles, woolen textiles, shoes, and the other mass-produced products of the laboring masses. Here was the solid, tangible substance of economic life. Boston was the seaport for the New England manufacturing complex and the provider of the financial, commercial, and other services that that complex required. The men of affairs looked at the manufacturing industries of neighboring New England and were gravely alarmed. They were in decline or potential decline. The cotton-textile industry was in mass flight to the Southern states. The woolen industry was poised for similar departure. Soon it would be the shoes and mass-produced artifacts that would go. The port of Boston was already beginning to show a seedy decline. The same would thereafter be the fate of its other supporting entrepôt services. The handwriting, old, enfeebled, but highly legible, was on the wall.

It could be erased only by drastic action. There should be tax reform and tax concessions to save the textile industries. Wages must be made competitive with the Carolinas and Georgia (admitting that these were pretty near starvation levels). Investment was needed in the port and its squalid ancillary facilities and structures. And a good tax climate was needed for other supporting services and industries. Were Boston and Massachusetts to continue to divert money and attention to Boston's public services—including, by implication, its top-heavy cultural, scientific, and educational estate—then very soon there would be no economic underpinning. All would collapse. The practical realities must be recognized. I do not think anyone who remembers the state of mind of thirty or forty years ago will seriously dispute my description of the diagnosis.

The recommendations of the practical men were not followed. And in a substantial measure their expectations were met. Cotton textiles, woolen textiles, shoes, and other products of good straightforward toil did move to the South or beyond the seas. The great red mills closed down or were converted to a variety of anonymous and undistinguished uses. The older industrial services of the city of Boston did decay. Soon it was hard to look at the wharves and the railroad stations and imagine that they had ever been used. But the somber expectations were not all fulfilled. The per-capita income of the city and the state continued to increase, enough so that it stayed among the highest in the country; it remained, needless to say, far higher than that of the Southern states to which the older industries had deserted. There was unemployment, but there was also much new employment. In contrast with other cities, the center of Boston did not decay. No commercial building now readily visible on the Boston skyline could have been seen there before World War II. Herein lies the lesson, backed by solid experience, on the future of Boston.

It is the deepest conviction of men who praise their practical common sense that industrial activity is man's ultimate economic frontier. It is not so. Once people are reasonably supplied with goods, they want them to be better or to work better. And they become concerned with how they look. And, above all, people give attention to where they themselves live. It is the activities that improve operational quality, artistic quality, and the ambience of living that take over and become important. It is this sequence that has saved Boston and Massachusetts, and will save us in the future.

In this sequence, the engineer and the scientist have a vital role, and so for that reason does the great scientific and engineering establishment of the Commonwealth. This has been greatly strengthened by the large additional expenditures made since World War II, which, among other things, have turned the University of Massachusetts from an underprivileged college of agriculture into one of the nation's leading state universities. But beyond science and engineering there are yet other frontiers. There is the provision of knowledge for its own sake; also the large artistic and aesthetic frontier; and finally, the services that enhance community life. Education and cultural activity become industries in their own right, for which people will pay. So does the direct enjoyment of painting, music, and the performing arts. And artistic achievement serves the desire, after things have been made to work, that they look good. The modern household has no appliance or gadget that wasn't invented thirty years ago. All recent change has been in miniaturization, modification, and, above all, improvement in visual design. In everyday consumer products, the designer, as distinct from the engineer, has become the decisive figure.

Thus we see how Boston and Massachusetts have been saved. We have hit upon the forms of economic development that are enjoyed, pay well, and have a future. No other part of the country has been so conscious of its educational, intellectual, and artistic preeminence. This preeminence serves the industry that seeks education for its own satisfaction. It serves also the industries that are based on engineering and scientific excellence. It has a strong symbiotic relation with design change and improvement. It attracts the large number of people untied to specific location who, in modern society, are deeply concerned with the quality of their surroundings; the current conventional wisdom to the contrary, these people pay only secondary attention to taxes and much more to the character of the community, the interest that it holds and serves, and the quality of the public services that are provided. Perhaps more than anything else, the prosperity of Massachusetts and other New England states has turned on their ability to attract this residential industry, as it may be called.

So I would judge the future of Boston and Massachusetts to be reasonably secure. There is a recognition that our strength lies in our educational and cultural estate and the ambience that causes people to want to live in close association with it. We have still with us the men of simple, forthright mind who would have kept us in the shoe business. They talk compulsively about high taxes in Massachusetts; they do not see that these pay for the institutions on which economic success depends. They would make tax concessions to retain industries that, under the best of circumstances, we shall one day lose. But I would judge that this view and these people are a temporary aberration, a useful reminder that as *La Garde meurt, mais ne se rend pas,* so also economic error. Our basic instinct is that sound policy still consists in making Boston—and Massachusetts—in the most complete possible sense, the best place in the Republic in which to live. We believe that if the people stay or come, the future follows. And so, happily, it is.

162 A BOOK FOR BOSTON

John Adams, oil on paper by an unknown artist, ca. 1800.
COLLECTION OF THOMAS BOYLSTON ADAMS

Stephanie, Elaine and Tony, dancers of the Boston Ballet, 1976. MARIE COSINDAS

164   A BOOK FOR BOSTON

Fifth floor of the Boston Athenaeum, 1979. JERRY L. THOMPSON

"Appeal to the Great Spirit" by Cyrus Dallin, erected in 1912 at the Museum of Fine Arts. LEE FRIEDLANDER

Poem for the Occasion

*Composed for the Centennial Celebration
of the Boston Museum of Fine Arts
and first read by the poet at the Centennial Dinner
given by the Museum, 4 February 1970.*

FOREWORD

David McCord's *Poem for the Occasion* appeared in print some ten years ago with an introduction by me and seemed to feel comfortable in the association—comfortable enough, in any case, to wish to repeat the excursion.

Which delights me because it gives me an opportunity to say for a second time that occasional poems—particularly occasional poems brave enough to say so—deserve more serious consideration than they get. All such a poem needs to turn it into poetry is a great occasion and a poet capable of recognizing greatness, and we have that combination here.

The occasion now is the three hundred and fiftieth anniversary of the founding of the city that was principally responsible for the American Revolution and even more responsible for the human and humane climate in which the great Republic grew.

And the poet is a man who has lived in that city since he discovered it from the other side of the Charles as an undergraduate, and who knows it now as well as he knows his art. Which is very well, indeed. For he has learned the great essential that in poetry—even in "occasional" poetry—it is the poem, not the poet, that speaks.

As I wrote ten years ago, this *Poem for the Occasion* is far more than that. It is, quite simply, a *poem*, through which, as through an astronomer's lens, relationships in spiritual space may be discerned. When they appear the occasion is transformed into the poem. And the city is said.

Archibald MacLeish
Conway, Massachusetts

Rogier van der Weyden: St. Luke Painting the Virgin
All photographs courtesy of Museum of Fine Arts, Boston

POEM FOR THE OCCASION

. . . only a stage in the endless
study of an existence, which is the
heroic subject of all study.
          WALLACE STEVENS

          I

Everybody is his own museum. We carry
in ellipsoid storage, each of us, impressions of
great art intuitively gathered, catalogued,
committed to the mind's retrieval system, with no
flashing lights or syllabus of IBM. Our
prime collection, winnowed as we add, shows
little that is unessential, bears no overhead
except the brain, makes do without solicited
endowment, upkeep, restoration; lends, borrows, and
exchanges nothing; rejects and correlates; all
periods distinct; all schools osmotic—
fluid, if we wish, as passing migratory
fish—Neandros to Brancusi, Lear Picassoesque,
Tolnec to Braque, one Hiroshige figure
clowning Prendergast. All this reciprocal and
retrospective in one sweep of summoned
galleries, or solitary as the Mona Lisa,

save "the glance that pierced to an
opposing soul." We have no visitors, no
light upon the paper, stone, bronze,
canvas but the inward eye. Nothing is
perfect, nothing near perfection: for
what image ever was? Yet we retain
triumphant passages, fine detail, brush-
strokes, shading, palette knife, patina,
scattered accents, melting values, as
uraeus on Egyptian deities, the curtal lip
that Gogarty describes.

Artist's model of limestone head
of Egyptian Queen

II

Say the word classic. Surely something Greek will
Spring to the mind: Euripides, blind Homer;
What every schoolboy knows about—one track man,
                              throwing the discus.

All the complexity of queer Greek letters
Long since resolved by sophomores on campus,
Keen for fraternal friendship; smeared Pi Sigmas
                              on rocks by thruways.

God! Are we Greek! Mellifluous Hymettus!
(Greek noun: the adjective, of course, is Latin.)
Where would we be without Hellenic root-words:
                              Alphabet, psyche,

Telephone, plastic, geometric, anchor,
Optical, thermos, symptom, pope, arthritis:
Symphony, pepper, atom, bomb—and get these:
                              buffalo, cactus.

Not just the weight of language. No, there's Plato,
Socrates, Euclid, Pindar, Sappho, others;
Pericles, yes; and names beyond this meter:
                              Hesiod, let's say.

Why in this country bankrupt our own language,
Sinewy, thonged with Greek? Thalassic wonder
Fused with good Anglo-Saxon: why debase it?
                              Speak in graffiti?

Still, there is something else: one language scarcely
Open to change—Greek art, a world up attic,
Perhaps the greatest trunkful outside Athens
                              right here in Boston.

Boston Museum—Greek word, note!—of Fine Arts.
"Grèce . . . mère des arts." (Musset said that.) Athena's
Temple an Athenaion (Athenaeum).
                              What could be neater?

Greece, the small country, large in philosophic
Dowery; larger still in architecture,
Amphoras, sculpture, bronzes, coins, gems, jewelry,
                              red-figure vases.

Nothing for me eclipses Aphrodite,
Given by Francis Bartlett; one spun lovely
Cup or a kantharos; that small gold earring
                              charioteering.

Marble for Aphrodite, and it suits her;
Head of Arsinoe a good close second;
Bronze (Perkins gift), thrice graceful
                    groovy cool Thracian!   Gold earring of winged Nike

Naming good people whom we hold beholden:
Donors, Curators—wise, alert collectors—
Should be the subject of unwritten strophes,
                                        over and over.

Yet does the artist choose to trace venation
Not of a hundred leaves to show the beech tree.
No! He will paint but one in isolation.
                                        This is called closure.

Poets do likewise. Edward Perry Warren
Fits my Greek meter; so does Lacey Caskey;
George Chase, great soul; Miss Wilbour—numismatics;
                                        Syracuse silver.

Warren brought Greece to Boston: benefactions
Bowdoin and Oxford, Harvard, also shared in.
Keats' hundredth birthday started him collecting:
                                        Coincidental.

Speaking of urns inspiring: queer, that sixteen
Stanzas are what I've turned. For Quiller Couch was
Half in my mind. His darling sapphics, "Lady
                                        Jane," are the same length.

    III

Before the time of the frog and water music,
Bashō and haiku, there were those Chinese
mountains underhung with mist, fledged with
arthritic trees, but capped by cheerful cloudfloats
fattening in dynastic blue. Japan, a chain of
islands catenary in volcanic space,
arranges somewhat like a disengaged ancestral
painting. She has made a cult of diminution,

being small. Oh, were the world still small that
we might sense this eloquence of space: dimension
in itself, not there to be annihilated. Haiku,
one small kite, flies by its lonesome clearly.
But, and I beg pardon, I employ this makeshift
stanza, since the accidental meter fits my
gracenotes to the richness of the Museum's
canton of Japan. Or do I light a string
of firefly lanterns as when I was very young?

My wise and witty
uncle lived in Japan two
    years. An engineer,

he collected art
of no importance, such as
    kakemonos, one

of which he gave me;
shards of language of the streets.
    Could it be true he

knew Lafcadio
Hearn? His kwannon leans my way,
    small feet on my desk.

Hiroshige, born
one hundred years before me,
    and my favorite

Hokusai were gone.
And Utamaro, Yoshu
    Chikanobu too;

Hiroshige: Shower on Ohashi Bridge

MCCORD *Poem for the Occasion*   173

but here they shine in
little frames I give them now
in retrospection

of that lovely land
prefigured long ago, one
reach of riches,

Honshu to our hand,
Stelligeri forever—
names of pioneers

like Fennollosa,
Morse, his neighbor; Bigelow,
Weld, and Denman Ross.

You may remember
Hearn writing Fennollosa?
"I can afford friends

only on paper."
So I murmur to myself,
Has that paper one

small figure out of
Hokusai, O then my sung
Museum in this

environs someone
said has nothing but dead past,
permits me voyage

where Henry Adams,
John LaFarge, and Percival
Lowell summered well.

I can seek my own
Nirvana and not worry,
    as the reporter did

who asked of John and
Henry: "Are you not rather
    late in the season?"

IV

Degas and Renoir, Monet and Manet:
So close in time, but no two pairs a pair.
These are my four, but how I cannot say.

Degas: Carriage at the Races

One flings confetti on a field of hay,
Rivers, cathedral: light that lingers there.
Degas or Renoir? Monet or Manet?

One of you praised the racetrack and ballet—
As I your portraits, I your landscapes, share.
These are your four, but how I cannot say.

One of you held his brushstroke poised to lay
The paint with swift yet velvet-kitten care,
Degas and Renoir, Monet and Manet.

One of you sang that singer on her way;
You—one to three—could Denman Ross not spare.
These are my four, but how I cannot say.

I stand in front of you. No one holds sway.
I turn the endless corners of a square.
Degas and Renoir, Monet and Manet:
These are my four, but how I cannot say.

Peto: The Poor Man's Store

V

The children come with decibels
And bounce them off the walls.
Into one room they swarm and zoom
Into another where Isis turns
Or Turner in his sunset burns.
The living aneurysm swells
With third-grade blood, but still the halls
Contain it. Nothing else is red
Except the hair on one small head:
A child absorbed by what enthralls.
What is it none but her discerns?
By light of revelation shed,
From Hippocrene the water wells,
Bells ring and she to art is wed.

VI

Persia! What lush and liquid words you trade:
Like taffeta, like julep. I invade
Bazaars, examine azure, lazuli,
Pistachio—green thought in my green shade.

Or else I walk the gallery to where
Your folded ibex meditates, more fair,
Adorable, than ten fine deities.
Of his bronze resignation I despair.

Not mine that finial of fantastic cats
With upward of three thousand years of spats
Behind them. I prefer the zebu bull:
Pottery Rhyton—boy! whatever that's!

Bronze Ibex

VII

Then drifting out through Asia on the wings
Fitzgerald gave The Rubáiyát, some things
Arrest me. I am free to pick and choose,
From art's demotic interface with kings,

Small trinkets here and there, for small things please.
One head of Buddha: basalt, Javanese.
That lovelier smiling head—Afghanistan;
Proud Chinese horse, T'ang dynasty. From these

To mini-micro carvings of one race:
All Japanese, all ivory, all grace.
Nétsuke: Small creatures of the earth—
Frogs, turtles, mice . . . Mirth . . . Wild uncommon-
     place.

A pile of seven turtles

I note elsewhere four Baryes. Why not more?
No Pompon. What a pity! Yet the store
Of animals is rich. My hippo bathes
In Kerma. And my birds are here galore.

Tapestries, textiles, give me little pause.
Ignorant of the loom, the weaver's laws,
I seek that Mughal carpet full of myth
And marvels, and admit wherein it awes.

But like all random journeys down great halls,
It is in Egypt that my own footfalls
Still echo last; where Horus puts to flight
Whole dynasties of dead centennials.

Travellers crowded in a ferry boat

Japanese Nétsuke are miniature sculptures in ivory or wood, used
as toggles to fasten a purse or box of incense or medicine to a
kimono sash. From the Bigelow collection, eighteenth and nineteenth centuries.

VIII

Nile is the river none can match for fame:
Euphrates, Tigris, Ganges, what you
        name : Name
One her length from tombs to crocodile—
Amazon? Mississippi? Still the Nile.

Praise Egypt, Reisner, Gardiner Martin Lane
That in this city gods and Nile Kings
        reign : Reign
In this pharaoh or 'great house'. Today's
Centennial strengthens with the sound of praise.

Small ibis cloisonné—New Kingdom bird;
Feathers blue paste, your weight in gold one-
        third : Third
Cataract perhaps your source. How tall
The pyramids! but you exquisite, small.

Gold and enamel ibis

IX

A museum, quite unlike a university,
grows by accretion: faculty unpensioned
and immortal on the walls, on pedestals, or
in glass cases. The older a museum, the likelier
grown in quality if not in size as well. Only
its director, scholars, and curators see the
college in it. Old citizen alumnus may not
owe it anything except the sole remembrance
of tired feet. Times haven't changed; for Plato
one-score-three, I think, centennials ago declared
the early bankruptcy of mind respecting
the pursuit of knowledge. Man, in paraphrase

of Jowett, simply seems to lack the will and
does not know the way. And yet to growing numbers
a museum is like a college and, if large enough,
a university: all visible, not otherwise, as James
once said of what he called true Harvard.
I have attended many, hold some undeserved
invisible degrees for themes unwritten: one
on Arnesby Brown, Tate Gallery; Carrière's
          great Daudet
and his Daughter; also Pompon in the Luxembourg—
So I revise the Pompon animalier thesis, for
the sculptor was apprenticed first in Dijon, 1870!

Then for the Dutch the Hague; the Nike
(Paris); the Rosetta stone, B. M.; and just inside
Great Russell Square, a dealer crammed with early
Edward Lears. And so to Chinese cricket cages,
Kansas City; Burchfield up in Utica; George
Bellows—yes, and Barye—down in Baltimore; one
Whistler out in Pittsburgh; museum architecture
(Omaha); the French school in Chicago; Dali's
Good-by in the National Museum and Dali in the
late Lord Beaverbrook's spruce gallery in New
Brunswick; Canadians in Montreal, the Frick
collection of Corot; "Mink Pond"—magnificent true
Homer—in the Fogg; the Brooklyn Sargents;
          Manship, north
in Andover; Cavell by Bellows (Springfield);
Worcester's Bensons; Wyeth down in Maine; and
          last those
far-off woods of J. B. C. Corot I walked through
once in my great-uncle's gallery—Pennsylvania;
I have not been to Italy or Spain. Poets do
like lists of things. So from my notebook now,
much more at home. . . .

Corot: Morning near Beauvais

MCCORD Poem for the Occasion   179

Carrière: Portrait of Verlaine

X

Sometimes we come for one thing: for a pair
of Rembrandts, for Verlaine by Carrière;

sometimes to pause and place a mental X
against the best of all Toulouse-Lautrecs.

Great painters and great schools need separate time.
Don't mix satiric Daumiers with sublime

Nativities, old furniture with Klee,
or let one room of Millets blind Millet.

No poem in celebration of this place
would take Fray Felix and describe that face,

as if El Greco in perhaps the best
of all his portraits thus far in the west

could be described or praised: he does not heed
one's praise. His pictures praise themselves. Indeed,

you need not know from what some style rebels.
"Dead Christ with Angels," Florentine, has spells

to cast; but no word said about it tells
just what it is. The secret always lies

between the object and beholder. Wise
as we profess to be in ways of art,

true recognition always takes the heart
as well as head. A skilled geometrist

may see in Feininger what you have missed.
For me, within those intersecting planes

I see strange lights on cosmic weathervanes;
it isn't what, but how the thing explains.

XI

Don't let the abstract whelm you with its waves,
queer creatures—bird with mask by Morris Graves;

Green mountains sprung by Marin out of shape,
Kandinsky playing scenic chess—or gape

at X eccentrics, Vasarely squares:
one always dares to look at him who dares.

Soulages, a divagate soul, at least invites
through verticals and bands. Afreet affrights;

and Bontecou's Mad Bird suggests not eggs,
but hip heroics on two unmatched legs.

Noguchi in pentelic marble twists
the Pantheon to arms bound at the wrists

and mortised to a capital as can
deflect the mind to classical Japan.

Bewilderness still Aliceland: surprise
is part the Cyclops' concentrate in eyes,

part strange notations, astigmatic screed.
Sanskrit is blindness if you cannot read.

Mirò: Child with Star

XII

Sails set, remember, Boston headed east.
Even late Prendergast was of the least

last interest to collectors at a time
when Egypt, Greece, the Orient were prime

rich hunting ground. Let someone else contrive
Eighteen-fifteen to Eighteen-sixty-five

as limits to a qualitative yield
of native primitives! The untilled field

remained untilled until the Russian-born
M. Karolik, where gun and powder horn,

axe, plow, and scythe had played a larger part
in wakening America than art,

uncovered, as a map you might unroll,
one instant ancestry: stark, stunning, droll.

Artistic ancestry, that is: the quest
was not for names, for schools; but east and west

for water colors, lithographs, prints, oils,
pen sketches, pencil drawings. Conan Doyle's

fast fiction-inquiries were on a par
with what the Karoliks uncovered far

afield: all pictures bought because they said,
not for who signed them: memories now dead—

Bierstadt: Storm in the Mountains

182   A BOOK FOR BOSTON

The country's pioneers, the vanished breed.
For every Catlin, Bierstadt, Bingham, Heade,

or Innes, hundreds fameless in this cache;
and placenames wilder than the Allegash.

XIII

Copleys and Stuarts ask the mind prepared,
as for old silver. Here the craftsmen shared

their gifts directly, look you in the eye.
You never hankered for a tankard. Why?

Look on that "Stand and Kettle"—Gabriel Sleath:
the craftsman up above and underneath.

Take English slipware—not perhaps your dish,
but here it is. Take kylix, ecuelle:

or you can pass them over, as you wish;
but in the names of things—one syllable—

a door may open. Or in decimal lights
one Whistler low in tone wakes oversights,

as music overtones. To enter where
Gauguin has placed a village, strands you there.

Harnet's and Peto's work is never done.
Hands off! But your eye's off, and that's the fun.

Old Postman Roulin half returns my stare.
I whisper "Il est cocu, le chef de gare."

Van Gogh: The Postman Roulin

MCCORD *Poem for the Occasion*   183

Homer foreshortens his great dory, but
Frank Benson's burin makes too short a cut.

Which spins me round the circle of these notes
as if at sea in half a dozen boats,

or tangled in a web of art as pure
as cracks on painting—French word, craquelure.

XIV

I come to prints, the very oldest store
of art in this Museum: enough and more

to make the name of Blake and Géricault,
of Dürer, Ingres, and Goya, did we know

naught else about them; Rembrandt, Copley, too;
Degas, Matisse, and Prendergast. How few

of these we ever seem to set apart!
But if I would gain access to one art,

no matter what, I would begin with prints,
the pure in line; and I would gladly rinse

my eyes of all the world-wide second-rate
in oils, and ask no better than one plate

as whole and unaffected as in that
blue brilliance of "The Letter" by Cassatt.

Cassatt: The Letter

XV

That rose-red city half as old as time
Lies buried in the dust; but who will say
She does not bloom again as in the rhyme
We half remember? Though the door was splay,

Its opening smaller as we shouldered in,
We have shut out so much of value nil
To find so much long lost that must have been
The praise of light that never crossed our sill.

So it is now: some Indo-artisan
Molded the clay, some painter with one stroke
Brushed the cool watchet blue; man after man
Fluted the marble. Or the morning broke

With sun on silver, on the rich brocades.
Knife took the wood, the matrix did receive:
Stone faceted, and dyes of all the shades
Of autumn blended. I could well believe

One master of world-ruins, one with pack,
Theodolite, and compass, has exposed
The buried past; that from one canvas-crack
Spring all the heads and landscapes unsupposed.

Head of Aphrodite

MCCORD *Poem for the Occasion*   185

A Boston Birthday Buffet

 MENU

FOR A BOSTON BIRTHDAY BUFFET

To begin with—
> Cotuit Oysters and Ipswich Steamer Clams
> Priscilla Weston's Duxbury Codfish Balls with Egg Sauce
> Terrines of Scallops and Sole Garnished with Codfish Tongues and Cheeks,
>   Fresh North Shore Shrimp, and Mussels from Rhode Island Waters
> Old-fashioned Gallups Island Lobster Stew

The main course—
> Roast Ribs of Beef, Boston
> Roast New England Country Hams
> Cauldrons of Boston Baked Beans
> Granny Potato Casseroles from Down East Maine
> Fresh Corn Puddings
> Salads of Boston Lettuce

The finale—
> Cranberry Sherbets
> Fresh Blueberry Charlottes
> Colonial Indian Puddings with Homemade Vanilla Ice Cream
> New England Apples and Vermont Cheddar Cheeses

> > Rumbrosia
> > Wines of the Region
> > Local Applejacks and Brandies

OPPOSITE: Martignetti Grocery Co., 84 Salem Street, North End, 187
December 22, 1933. THE BOSTONIAN SOCIETY

Boston is a great food town, and always has been. To visitors prattling of the restaurants of New Orleans and San Francisco, I always say, "Have a look at our markets, and a taste of our home cooking." From the beginning of our history, we've had matchless ingredients close at hand, and market men say we're fastidious shoppers. The best beef in the country is shipped to Boston; we can choose from the freshest fish; we want our vegetables picked small and young; we like our eggs brown; we know our apples (you won't see the crisp, winy old varieties, like the Russets and Northern Spies, in markets anywhere else). In colonial and Federal times, the morning marketing was a stately ritual undertaken by the father of the family. Even the merchant princes were present, attended by servants, who would be sent home with the bundles and baskets while the nabobs proceeded downtown to their counting-houses. In an early book addressed to beginners in domestic service, Robert Roberts, butler to Nathan Appleton and to Governor Christopher Gore, describes such outings, offering some very good shopping hints and a few recipes notable for their refined simplicity and their insistence on freshness and quality.

Good food, yes indeed; clever food, no. Because of our long winters and short growing season, Boston cooks always had to devote more ingenuity to preserving food than to presenting it. Another reason was the constant need to provision long sea voyages and overland explorations in country one couldn't "live off": no wonder we became so adept with salt meats and fish, "portable soup" (meat glaze), pickles, fruit "butters" and jellies, maple sugar, dried ground corn, hard candy, hard cheese, mincemeat, sea biscuit, hard cider, applejack, beer—things that keep. The icehouse, the smokehouse, the cellar, and the larder mattered more in early New England than the kitchen, which was at first more of an all-purpose workshop and gathering place than a shrine of fine cooking. Remember the domestic tragedy in *Little Women* when Meg's bridegroom unexpectedly brought a friend home for dinner, only to find poor Meg in the throes of a day's jelly making? (But remember, too, that when the penurious March family gave a party, they thought nothing of ordering a lobster—doubtless a ten- or fifteen-pounder at a few pennies a pound!)

Kitchen wisdom then was a family thing, handed down along with the iron kettle and the butter churn. We had few professional cooks in our first two centuries, though our early settlers came from a culture in which a "household" often meant a palace, monastery, castle, barracks: a populous, hierarchically organized unit, where fine divisions of labor were possible. (Since the Middle Ages, Europe had had very specialized cooks' guilds). By the time of the Revolution, the Southern states had plantations of institutional size; but house by house, New England cooks were on their own.

Fannie Farmer's precise measurements and step-by-step recipes, along with post–Civil War prosperity and turn-of-the-century Anglophilia, were to change all that. In the manorial summer houses of Boston merchants, one saw cold rooms big enough for sides of beef, ranks of ice-cream wells, pastry marbles yards square, coal stoves the size of a concert grand, manned by large staffs and presided over, often as not, by a graduate of the Boston Cooking School: a person of consequence. In large houses and small, the high ceremony of the dinner party—with dishes passed in courses, not spread all over the table—became opulent indeed. Nancy Hale's *A New England Girlhood* has an unforgettable child's-eye glimpse from the head of the stairs: the ladies with their fascinatingly cleft décolletages, the climactic moment of the glistening iced pudding. But more poignant to old Bostonians is her memory of S. S. Pierce's wagon jolting up a summery lane, laden, especially, with gold-crested boxes of those crisp, snow-white peppermint wafers—the thought of them has the evocative power of Proust's madeleine. Order, seemliness, simplicity, exquisite quality: that was Boston housekeeping, and Boston cookery.

Lately, our fare has become eclectic, and we seem to be turning into a city of good restaurants. Dining out, or at someone's house, you may be offered anything from couscous to hairy melon; but for this birthday buffet, it seems only fitting to feast on indigenous dishes, recipes for a number of which are included here.

There has to be rum, of course, staple of the Triangle Trade and comfort of sailors. On his staircase landing, Harrison Gray Otis daily caused to be set out, and replenished as needed, an enormous bowl of rum punch for the heartening of visitors, help, and family passing up or down. In perpetuation of his hospitable spirit, we start with Rumbrosia, a new but reminiscent cocktail.

Then on to a fishy first course, where we really shine. I doubt better oysters than Cotuits exist, so they're a must. (Edward Weeks, of *The Atlantic*, once wrote that on Charles Dickens's first visit to America, his Boston hosts naturally proffered Cotuits, already world-famous. These were chosen for their size.

A respectful silence prevailed while the great man struggled with his first. Then he was asked how he felt. "Profoundly grateful," he gasped, "and as though I had just swallowed a small baby.") We look to the North Shore, Ipswich for choice, for our steamers, so good with a cup of simmering broth and the contrast of cold white wine; then down to Duxbury for a family recipe for codfish balls, unchanged since colonial days.

Though my family lived in California, my New England mother insisted on using Gorton's salt cod, all the way from Gloucester; I can still smell the raw wood of the flat box and the sharp oceany tang. Mother liked the hard codfish slabs to be thoroughly soaked, so she laid them in cold water on Friday noon, made her mixture on Saturday night, and had it all ready for cooking on Sunday morning. These codfish balls are lighter and fresher-tasting than most.

◢ A BOSTON BIRTHDAY COCKTAIL—RUMBROSIA

For 6 cocktails

1½ cups Noilly Prat dry French
    vermouth
⅔ cup dark Jamaica rum (Myers's)
4 tb Rose's sweetened lime juice

12 drops Angostura bitters
24 large ice cubes
6 strips of fresh orange peel

Stir the vermouth, rum, lime juice, and bitters in a pitcher and refrigerate until cocktail time. Place 4 ice cubes in large, handsome, stemmed wine glasses, and divide the drink among them, decorating each with a strip of orange peel, first rubbed around the rim of the glass, then dropped into it.

◢ PRISCILLA WESTON'S DUXBURY CODFISH BALLS
WITH EGG SAUCE

For 4 cups of codfish mixture, making about 4 dozen 1½-inch pieces

1 lb of salt cod (1 or more pieces)
1 smallish onion, thinly sliced
4 peppercorns
1 bay leaf
2 cups firm plain mashed potatoes

Salt and white pepper to taste
2 "large" eggs, beaten with a pinch of
    salt
1½ to 2 qt very fresh frying oil in a
    deep-fat fryer or 3-qt saucepan

Soaking the codfish. Cut it into ½-inch slices. Wash the slices in cold water, and set on a rack in a large bowl of cold water (slicing the fish makes it soak faster, and the rack keeps it out of the salt that falls to the bottom of bowl). Refrigerate the soaking slices, changing the water once or twice, until fish feels fresh, and tastes hardly of salt—a good 24 hours.

Poaching the codfish. Simmer the sliced onion, pepper, and bay leaf for 5 minutes in 2 cups of water, then add 2 more cups of water and the soaked fish, adding more water if necessary to cover it. Bring to the simmer, cover the pan, remove from heat, and let stand for 10 minutes, or until you are ready to use it. (Simmering or boiling toughens salt cod.)

The codfish mixture. Drain the codfish, reserving cooking liquid for the sauce. Flake the fish into a mixing bowl, and beat in the mashed potatoes, using a wooden spoon or an electric mixer (not a food processor, which will grind it; you want it shredded). Beat in ¾ of the beaten eggs, plus a little more if mixture is very stiff. Beat in salt and pepper to taste. (You may wish to let mixture stand at room temperature for half an hour or so, to firm up a little as it cools, making for easier forming.)

(*) Ahead-of-time note: May be made in advance. Cover and refrigerate when cool, and beat up briefly before using.

Frying the codfish balls. Shortly before serving, heat frying oil to 375°F, and heat oven to 200°F. Line a pizza tray or jelly-roll pan with several thicknesses of paper towels. When oil is at the right temperature, scoop up 1½-tablespoon balls of codfish mixture with a soup spoon, and dislodge into the hot fat with a rubber spatula, making them as round as possible—but the rather rough shape with shreds of codfish protruding gives a light and crisp result. Fry 4 to 5 at a time, for 2 or 3 minutes, or until nicely browned. Remove with a skimmer to the paper-lined tray, and keep warm in the oven. Serve as soon as possible, with the following egg sauce.

Leftover-codfish note. If you don't want to make the full 48 codfish balls, you may freeze the unformed mixture, or turn it into a codfish chowder just by heating it up with enough milk to make a soupy mixture—any remains of the following sauce could be stirred into it, too.

◪ EGG SAUCE TO SERVE WITH CODFISH BALLS

For about 2½ cups of sauce

4 tb butter
4 tb flour
2 cups hot codfish-poaching water, strained

2 hard-boiled eggs, chopped
Salt and white pepper to taste
1 to 2 tb additional butter or several tb heavy cream (optional)

Melt the butter in a heavy-bottomed saucepan, blend in the flour, and cook, stirring, over moderately low heat until flour and butter foam and froth together for 2 minutes without turning more than a buttery yellow. Remove from heat, and when bubbling has stopped pour in all of the hot liquid at once, beating vigorously to blend. Bring to the boil and simmer, stirring, for 2 minutes. Fold in the chopped eggs, and salt and pepper to taste. (If not to be used shortly, film surface with a little milk, cream, or butter.) Just before serving, reheat, then remove from heat and stir in the optional butter or cream.

It used to be hard to obtain codfish tongues and cheeks, sometimes called "sounds," for the crews on the fishing boats ate them all up before returning to port; indeed, they are a great delicacy, and I remain in grateful ignorance as to why one can buy them now. Sliced, poached, and set around a mousse of fish baked in a terrine, they make a charming garnish, interspersed with fat, peach-pink mussels from the Rhode Island shore and small, rosy shrimp from Gloucester. Sole for the mousse can be our gray or lemon sole (or use halibut). For scallops, one might go to Chatham, where the creatures flap and clap over the bay waters, winking their rows of mad blue eyes.

For lobsters to make stew, we need go no farther than our own outer harbor. The following recipe is named to commemorate long-gone delights: on uninhabited Gallups Island, embowered in wild roses and honeysuckle, stand the spacious, deep foundations of an old summer hotel; even before its Victorian day, the island was farmed, so we may assume that thick, golden cream was available for a perfect stew, with lobsters taken from the clean shoal waters nearby, at that spot, out beyond the airport, where the real sea winds and sea smells begin.

If you're "banting," as people used to call dieting, have a fine fresh boiled lobster with a bit of lemon. But a proper stew needs plenty of butter and cream, because they absorb and distribute the pure, intense lobster flavor throughout the liquid, and every mouthful is then a divine sensation. Besides its marvelous taste, a stew is a clever way of making two small lobsters serve six people.

◢ OLD-FASHIONED GALLUPS ISLAND LOBSTER STEW

Timing note—a lobster stew needs time to cure; plan to make it a day or even 2 or 3 days before serving it. For 6 people

2 freshly boiled 1¼- to 1½-lb live lobsters
1½ sticks (6 oz) unsalted butter
Salt and freshly ground white pepper to taste

1½ qt milk, or part milk and part medium or heavy cream in such proportions as you deem wise (see manufacturing note at end of recipe)
3 tb additional butter, chilled

Preparing the lobsters. Remove all the meat from the lobsters, being careful to leave the meat from 3 of the large claws whole. Slice the meat of these 3 claws in half horizontally, to give the appearance of 6 pieces of claw meat; reserve them until serving time. Cut the tail meat (after removing intestinal veins) into crosswise slices ½-inch thick. Collect all the tomalley (green matter), coral (if any), and the white matter clinging to the inside of the shells, and force it through a sieve into a bowl. Discard stomach sacks from inside the head part of the shells. Chop shells into ½-inch pieces.

Lobster stock from shells. In a heavy-bottomed saucepan, over moderately high heat, sauté the lobster shells in 4 tablespoons of the butter, stirring about frequently, for 3 to 4 minutes. Pour in just enough water to cover the shells, bring to the boil, cover the pan, and simmer for 10 minutes. Then raise heat and boil rapidly until liquid is reduced to about ½ cup. Strain it into the milk. (The shells give added flavor and color to the stew.)

Sautéing the lobster. Meanwhile, in a heavy-bottomed 3-quart saucepan, melt 4 tablespoons of butter over moderate heat. In the melted butter simmer the sieved lobster-tomalley mixture, stirring with a wooden spoon for 5 to 6 minutes, until mixture turns brownish red. Add 4 more tablespoons of butter and, when butter is melted, stir in the lobster meat (except the reserved claw pieces). Sauté slowly, stirring gently, for 7 to 8 minutes; lobster will gradually turn a nice salmon pink. Remove from heat and let cool to tepid.

Adding the liquids. Heat the milk and cream to tepid, to about the same temperature as the lobster. Then, by small dribbles, as though you were making a mayonnaise, begin ladling the milk into the lobster meat, stirring all the while as the milk mixture absorbs the salmon pink of the lobster. Cover and refrigerate for

24 hours at least; the milk, cream, and lobster must have time together for the lobster flavor to permeate the liquid.

Serving. Bring the stew slowly to the simmer and maintain at the barest simmer for 2 to 3 minutes. Taste, adding salt and white pepper as you think needed. Ladle into hot soup bowls, topping each serving with a slice of chilled butter on which you place a reserved piece of claw meat. Accompany with toasted common crackers, or pilot biscuits, or toasted and buttered English muffins (a modern touch, but a happy one).

Manufacturing note. I have noticed, when I use mostly milk rather than mostly medium cream for my stew, that however careful I am to add it slowly to the lobster, a layer of lobster-pink butter rises and coagulates on the surface of the stew as it chills. The solution is to scrape the butter off, heat it in a saucepan, and stir in 2 tablespoons of flour. Cook slowly for 2 minutes, remove from heat, and whisk in by dribbles 1½ cups of lobster liquid. Simmer for 2 minutes, fold it into the rest of the stew, and bring to the simmer just before serving. A light thickening like this is also a plus when your stew is of spartan milk rather than rich and heavy cream.

Our main course is as hearty, plain, and soul-satisfying as a speech by Leverett Saltonstall, of recent and beloved memory. Roast beef, of course, to remind us of the traditional Boston Sunday lunch, eaten after a two-hour sermon in the odor of sanctity (which I take to be lavender water) and worked off that afternoon by the four-mile-an-hour constitutional referred to by hardy Brahmins as a little stroll. For a fine smoked country ham, we needn't look to the South. The best one I ever tasted was served by the poet Peter Davison at his salt-marsh farm in Gloucester; each year he fattens two pigs, which are then butchered, and the hams smoked, by an ancient firm of experts in Groton. They salt the best of the fat, rind on (being gelatinous, pork rind gives body to a sauce), to be used in chowders and, particularly, in baked beans. Here's a modern version of the classic Boston baked beans, done in a slow cooker.

Our potato recipe is a very old one, and so useful I wish the unknown Maine-coast grandmother who created it could be honored by name. So few potato dishes can be made way ahead of time for a big party, but this one doesn't mind sitting on a warming tray while guests come and go.

BOSTON BAKED BEANS IN A SLOW-COOKING ELECTRIC POT

For about 2 quarts of baked beans

1 lb (2 cups) small white beans
5 cups water
6 oz (¾ cup) diced or sliced salt pork,
    simmered 10 minutes in 1 qt of water,
    and drained (include the pork rind
    too, if you wish)
1½ tsp salt

1 cup finely sliced onion
1 to 2 cloves garlic, minced (optional)
3 tb dark unsulfured molasses
2 tb Dijon-type prepared mustard
½ tb grated fresh ginger (optional)
Pepper to taste

Pick over and wash the beans. Mix everything in the slow cooker, put on the lid, and turn heat to high until contents are bubbling. Turn to low, and cook 14 to 16 hours or longer (turning heat to high once or twice if beans do not seem to be cooking). Beans are not done until they have turned a nice darkish reddish brown. Correct seasoning.

Note: There are many strong opinions on what flavors Boston baked beans should have: some add tomatoes, others omit onions, and so forth and so on. I happen to favor these seasonings, but there is no law!

GRANNY POTATOES FROM DOWN EAST MAINE

For 12 to 14 people

12 medium-size "boiling" potatoes
    (3 lb)
Salt

For 4½ cups of sauce:

4 cups milk, heated in a saucepan
1 stick (¼ lb) butter
½ cup all-purpose flour (measure by
    scooping dry-measure cup into flour
    and sweeping off excess)
2 large cloves of garlic, minced or
    puréed

1 tb butter
½ to ⅔ cup coarsely grated Vermont
    cheddar cheese

1 tsp curry powder
1 tb prepared mustard (preferably the
    imported kind with mustard grains
    in it; or Dijon-type mustard)
White pepper and drops of hot pepper
    sauce

Equipment: A 4-qt saucepan for boiling the potatoes; a heavy 2-qt pan for the sauce; a wooden spatula or spoon; a wire whip; a rubber spatula; a 2½- to 3-qt shallow baking and serving dish, such as a round one 12 inches in diameter and 2 inches deep.

The sauce. Heat the milk. Meanwhile, in the 2-quart saucepan, melt the butter, blend in the flour, and stir with a wooden spoon or spatula over moderate heat until butter and flour foam and froth together for 2 minutes without turning more than a buttery yellow. Blend in the garlic and curry, and remove from heat. When bubbling has stopped, vigorously blend in ½ the hot milk with your wire whip, then the rest, beating until smooth. Set over moderately high heat and stir with whip until sauce comes to the boil; boil slowly, stirring, for 2 to 3 minutes. Beat in the mustard, then several grinds of pepper and 4 or 5 drops of hot pepper sauce. Taste very carefully for seasoning, adding a little more mustard if you think it necessary. Sauce should be quite thick; if too thick, thin out by beating in droplets of milk.

Assembling. Smear a tablespoon of butter inside the baking dish, and spread in a thin layer of sauce. Over it arrange ⅓ of the potatoes, and over them ⅓ of the cheese. Reserving ⅓ of the sauce for the end, spread ½ the remaining sauce over the potatoes. Continue with another layer of potatoes, cheese, and sauce, ending with the layer of the potatoes, the reserved sauce, and the final amount of cheese.

(*) *Ahead-of-time note:* May be prepared a day in advance to this point; when cool, cover with a sheet of plastic wrap and refrigerate.

Baking and serving. About half an hour before serving, set in the upper third level of a preheated 425°F oven until contents are bubbling and cheese topping has browned nicely.

(*) *Ahead-of-time note:* May be kept warm, uncovered, on an electric warming device, or over hot water; do not let the potatoes overheat or actually cook, or they will dry out.

Fattening note. I usually make mine with low-fat milk, but your conscience must be your guide here, because a sauce made with light cream is delicious indeed.

No need to think of this as a seasonal menu, since you can make corn pudding from market corn on the cob, available all year round; it doesn't have to be fresh-picked. And while nothing can equal a crisp, rustling head of Boston lettuce fresh from the garden, this elegant salad green has become so popular you can get it any time, imported from goodness knows where. But it would be nice, on a summer morning, to pick wild blueberries for the charlottes, up on the gentle, sunny slopes of the Sagamore Hills, near Essex. Perfect for blueberries, it's hardscrabble country, with the underlying granite rubbing through the thin topsoil, and the growth reverting to scrub and sumac and juniper; it seems unimaginable, but the old stone walls tell us this land must once have been farmed. Maybe, 350 years hence, future Bostonians will find the forest resurgent there. Maybe, if "small is beautiful" still, they'll farm it Indian style, grubbing out little clearings to grow corn, to dry and grind for pudding!

Colonial Indian pudding is lovely with vanilla ice cream, which Boston households were serving long before refrigeration was taken for granted elsewhere—we never did lack for ice, or sawdust to pack it in. (The purest ice in the world, it was once thought, came from sparkling little Wenham Lake; as Kipling tells, it was exported even as far as India.) Nowadays, ice cubes, with sweetened cooked cranberries, turn into sherbet after a two-minute spin in a food processor—and thus is struck the note of innovation that should punctuate every Boston party.

For another novelty—soon, let us hope, to be part of our tradition—note that the standard menu phrase "wines of the region" is no longer a local joke. Down at Sakonnet Vineyards in Little Compton, Rhode Island—a lovely village, silvery with sun-bleached meadows, mica-bright stone walls, and weathered shingles, all shawled in June with rambler roses—Jim and Lolly Mitchell are producing elegant wine. It hasn't the "foxy" taste East Coast wines used to; this is the real thing, subtle and fine, well worthy of a celebration like this one. Wine to sip and sniff and savor. But the feast should end in traditional style—remember, the Puritans were perfect soaks—so let's raise a glass of sound old applejack to our town and its next 350 years, and toast it with three times three: cheers, though, not glasses, for Bostonians always wind up safe at home.

"Apple Mary," Boston Common, ca. 1860.
MASSACHUSETTS HISTORICAL SOCIETY

OPPOSITE: Jamaica Pond Ice Co. wagon, ca. 1900. Photograph by Charles Currier.
THE BOSTONIAN SOCIETY

High Rationale

There are those who say Boston's prime evils
  Are the high-rising Pru and the Hancock,
But all cities suffer upheavals:
  There are skyscrapers even in Bangkok.

True, the structures of hundred-odd storeys
  Block our view of the gold State House dome
That was one of the principal glories
  For the many who call Boston home,

Still, the Hancock, though frequently twitted
  Till its defenestration had ended,
Now shines forth, it must be admitted,
  Pellucid and utterly splendid.

"It's a constant delight to the viewer,"
  As someone was recently saying,
"And if the old vistas are fewer,
  Well, that is the price I. M. Pei-ing."

Copley Square, 1974. NICHOLAS NIXON

Boston University Chapel and Plaza on Commonwealth Avenue, 1979. JERRY L. THOMPSON

Boylston Street, with the old and new buildings of the Boston Public Library at the right, 1979. JERRY L. THOMPSON

Cambridge River Festival, 1978. NICHOLAS NIXON

Nantasket Beach, Hull, 1977. NICHOLAS NIXON

Commonwealth Avenue, 1975. TOD PAPAGEORGE

Bringing George Home

She is coming home with George: George is six and has never been home before. For him it is an odyssey into the future and for her, a pilgrimage into the past.

There are some—and she is one of them—who think that you can't really get to Boston anymore now that the South Station is for all intents and joyous purposes gone, and the great portal that opened upon the hum and hustle of the city is boarded up. You arrived there from Chicago and New York and from the towns on the South Shore, into the giant echoing cavern of the station, dark and smelling of coal smoke and of adventure. It was fine to be on a Pullman with your luggage in the aisle, the green plushy seats dusty from your sojourn and the redcaps waiting, but even if you were coming in from Hingham on your way to Crawford Hollidge or to Jordan Marsh, you never heard the conductor call "Back Bay!" without that mounting tension: *fun*.

George feels the same way coming into Logan. He has never been on a plane before and says that it is "wicked," by which he means what she meant: *fun*. Dipping down over the gentle hills, so many of them wooded, they see for an instant the thick stone needle of the Bunker Hill monument and ahead, the tall young buildings lifting smoke-colored and blue windows into an azure sky. There are not so many of them yet that they cramp one another, but stand separate and clean-shouldered above the humped-dowager edifices and the cobbled streets and tangled lanes that are home.

When parents are peripatetic, and scattered families are but loosely strung on the potential thread of airlines, everyone wants the children to know home. She wants George to know the place to which and from which his forebears came: the Athens of America, the Hub, the city where the intellect is still more honored in the observance than in the breach, where you walk with the past as comfortably as with a neighbor.

They leave their luggage; their friend will help them to redeem it later. She well remembers when nobody went to Boston without hats and gloves, but today she wears sneakers and swings a canvas tote bag that contains all they will need for the day. George, like all proper boys, wears jeans and jersey and full shiny hair above big, round bright eyes. She is comfortable enough: they are bound to see those whose dress is at once more extravagant and less formal than their own; already this year, some of the young will be barefooted.

They can take a bus to the subway, but if they do they are going to rattle past the stop for the new Aquarium; she is as partial to aquariums as the next and would like to see the giant sea turtles sliding by. But like the Science Museum and the Fine Arts, it will have to wait. This is a day for out-of-doors: May, summer's morning, and a sky that cradles the city in clean, blue arms.

They take a cab. "Faneuil Hall," she says.

The "cradle of liberty" was given to Boston by Peter Faneuil, who traded in slaves, and here during the Revolution the patriots assembled. It used to be dwarfed and stunted, pushed in upon by the city, but now it stands free and fair again, flanked by the bright refurbished markets: North, South, and Faneuil. George does not know what a patriot is, and she is not sure she wants him to know yet. When he does, she will take him to Bunker Hill and to Concord and Lexington and to Faneuil Hall. But today she is looking for a kite. If it is exotic, aromatic, or edible, you can find it at the markets, and they buy a scarlet beauty sculptured like a bird.

George is worried. He asks, "Can you fly a kite?"

No. But she is not worried. There are always nice young people on the Common walking their dog or carrying their baby in a backpack, who are glad to help a small boy get his kite up or down.

Before they cross Tremont Street she looks down toward Boylston to the corner where the Touraine Hotel used to be. It was there that her mother decided to marry her worldly father because he flamed brandy in his coffee and carried a press card to prove he was the correspondent from Boston College to *The Boston Globe*. He was nineteen and about to leave with the Massachusetts State Guard for Mexico, but not before he wired her, "Off to the front." Another year and he would be off with the A.E.F. to another front in France.

This is the sort of thing she wishes George to know, because, someday, he will want to tell his son.

The Common is at its best. The last forsythia still froths and the magnolia foams; the grass gives off that hot, new smell and is buttoned with dandelions. The Common sweetens the memories of wars. They climb the little knoll and pay tribute to the Union dead, although George does not know about the Union, either, and they stand in silence before the Saint-Gaudens upon which, in low relief, the black troops march perpetually to the Civil War. Then in the open spaces while a new friend helps George mount his kite, she peoples the Common with the crowds that gathered here on the day of the true Armistice.

Her mother wore a brimmed hat with a feather, that day in 1918, her coat was cinched in at the waist and her high-buttoned boots were two-colored, as if she wore spats. Strangers hugged one another and blew horns and, for some reason, flung talcum powder. Everyone seemed to be there and rejoicing. But of course, all over Boston there were silent homes to which the boys did not come back.

George is a philosophic child. His grandmother watches in dismay while the kite drifts up and away and over the gold helmet of the State House, but George is ready to move on. He skips beside her.

At Charles Street they look across to the iron gates of the Garden, and the balloon man is there, and the popcorn vendor with his hot, buttery bags. While they wait for the traffic to hesitate she remembers that her own grandmother bought her balloons here, the good kind that tug against the wind and not the kind that bob on the end of a thin wand. Her grandmother was a good friend. When she was past balloons, her grandmother went with her on the trolley along Huntington Avenue to see again at the Fine Arts the

Cézanne of the miraculous knife and the blue tablecloth and apple, and then to the little shops that sold art supplies, where you bought paints and charcoal and small, articulated wooden figures, because she had decided to be a painter, which did not turn out to be a good idea.

It was on Charles Street, too, that she and her young husband had their first apartment. It was a fourth-floor walk-up over an antique shop; you bought firewood by the stick and carried it up. Charles Street does not change much. The faint fragrance of wood fires still drifts about the roofs, and from the rows of houses with common walls young people still stride forth in the morning, walking to work. Around the corner on Beacon Street and in high, narrow quarters is Little, Brown and Company, Publishers.

Boston is also called the City of Books. Bostonian children are early aware of this, because they are on all sides surrounded by statues and monuments that commemorate the authors all America reveres, and by those august persons' actual homes. They may, in awe, visit the Longfellow house and that where Emerson lived, so close to the rude bridge that arched the flood, and they may gaze at the very costumes in which the Little Women played *Pilgrim's Progress* and at "Amy's" drawings, glassed and hanging on the woodwork and the walls. And then, everyone's grandmother has a bust of Dante and a full set of the *New England Poets*, and the children are encouraged to keep journals and to lisp in numbers if the numbers come. George's great-grandfather wrote books and so did his granduncle, and his grandfather and grandmother, too, and many of their friends, so that his own father as a little boy had asked, "But doesn't everyone?"

There are other fine publishers in Boston, but to her Little, Brown is also home.

George is possessive of his books, though he thinks they are written in faraway climes and probably by machines. It will be a long time before he tackles his grandfather's ten novels or his grandmother's nine, but he is familiar with *Make Way for Ducklings*, and at the Duck Pond is at home in Zion and not surprised to see the mothers swimming proudly while their little ones bob in their wake like bathtub toys. When they have slowly floated about behind the great white wooden swan, she looks wistfully across Arlington Street at the Ritz-Carlton, where the blue flag with its gilt lion's head swings lazily in a warm breeze. But small boys do not take much to hotels and the Ritz considers some things inappropriate to the Ritz; perhaps little boys are among them.

Anyway, it is suitable to picnic. In May, grandmothers picnic all over Boston with the children: on the Common, in the Arnold Arboretum, in Franklin Park, along the Esplanade, on all the gold and grassy margins of the Charles, and in the tote bag there are sandwiches made early, early, and far north of Portland. Perhaps one day George will say, "Upon this very spot, my grandmother did not lunch at the Ritz."

Presently, with a cupcake in each hand, he wanders off to make friends with a black little girl whose long-legged mother is reading in the sun.

Watching his striped straight back and his superb assurance, she thinks of another boy born long ago in Poverty Lane with a passion for learning, who left school at fourteen to work in a shoe factory. With his own kind of superb assurance, that boy would not believe doors would not open to one who would "gladly lerne and gladly teche"; his principal gave him books and lesson plans and made it possible for him to help his family, while, night after weary night, he earned his diploma and then went on to Bridgewater State Normal School. Ten years later he was himself the master of a Boston school and ten years after that was called across the river and was for thirty years Superintendent of Cambridge City Schools. During those years he earned seven honorary degrees and a certain amount of criticism, because, remembering his own broken boots, he rang out school too often on too many stormy days: there are still children who do not have boots. George's great-great-grandfather was a good and gentle man, who took recalcitrant boys into his own home to live with his own sons before he would see them in reform school, and someday she will take George to see the school named after him and where his portrait hangs: M. E. Fitzgerald.

But now the shadows of the iron fence fall one way and not the other. It is strangely quiet here at the heartwood of the city; even the traffic on Arlington Street is muted, and one hears the afternoon move in the new leaves. Decisions must be made. Shall it be Mrs. Jack Gardner's Palace? She herself would very much like to see again the Giorgione head of Christ carrying the cross, before which Mrs. Jack wanted violets always to be kept. George will be quickly bored with pictures that he has not colored, but he will like the balconies, the garden that astonishingly blossoms all year in the dead center of the ornate building, and he will think that the towering skylights are solar heating, which, come to think of it, of course they are.

No. There will be other days and things he will like better when he is seven. So they will go to F. A. O. Schwarz and let him choose a souvenir and then walk on and over to Copley Square, which is a place where she must always go. At Schwarz's he chooses a wooden circus that she would rather like to have herself, and is singularly reasonable when he learns it must go home by United Parcel. So she is reasonable too, and gets him a ball that he can carry in his pocket or his hand.

At Copley he is more impressed than she expected by the gigantic black-glass building that reflects the clouds passing and, like an evil Gulliver, menaces little Trinity Church below, and even diminishes the vast pile of the Boston Public Library. George pays no attention to the stone gentleman in the baggy granite pants who guards the church, but rather stands with his hands locked behind him looking way, way up at that black, gleaming ogre until she hopes it will not threaten his dreams tonight.

The steep concrete arena that is now the center of the square is made for boys and balls. While he plays, she finds a bench and quietly contemplates the roster that adorns the library like laurel: Copernicus, Galileo, Archimedes. Aeschylus, Sophocles, Euripedes. Homer, Tasso, Pindar. . . . *thick as autumnal leaves that strow the brooks in Vallombrosa,* . . . .

Hawthorne, Melville, Thoreau. The names of the noble dead. To be a citizen of a community that honors them is an honor.

They meet their friend at Number One, Boston Place. George has been in elevators before, but not one that takes him in a twinkling up forty floors. For the first time all day he wants his grandmother's hand and holds it as they stand at the great window, looking out. He says it is higher than the airplane; that is because you see more and what you see stays in place.

Far in the distance the Blue Hills are folded like quilts in the late, gentle light. South Boston stretches to their right. Below them but beyond is Boston Harbor, where the wharves bite into the blue. Nearer, and little and very dear, is the Custom House Tower, under which she and her uncle once met an old man who wanted to know how M. E. was and was glad to hear he was well. Moved by some ancient kindness or courtesy and searching for the words to say what he felt, he said, "We'll give him the biggest funeral the town's ever seen!"

And they did, George. They did.

When she went up with her uncle in the Custom House Tower they did so because it was the highest building in the city. Now it is knee-high to the hard new giants. But it is there. O city blessed with vision for the future, but proud custodian of the past! She holds the child's hand tightly. May he speak as Marcus Tullius Cicero.

Civis Romanus sum.

First Church of Christ, Scientist, 1975. Mother Church built by Franklin J. Welch in 1894; Christian Science Center built by I. M. Pei in 1973. NICHOLAS NIXON

THE CONTRIBUTORS

A native New Yorker, ANNE BERNAYS has lived in "Cambridge 02138" since 1959. She is the author of five novels (including *The First to Know* and *Growing Up Rich*) and many magazine articles and book reviews; her sixth novel, *The School Book*, will be published shortly. Bernays is president of P.E.N./New England. She and her husband, fellow-contributor Justin Kaplan, have three daughters.

JAMES CARROLL's most recent novel, *Mortal Friends*, was a best seller in both its hardcover and paperback editions. He is the author of an earlier novel, *Madonna Red*, and of several books of nonfiction. Carroll and his wife, Alexandra Marshall, also a novelist, live on Beacon Hill.

JULIA CHILD, whose cookbooks and TV cooking shows have won her a host of devotees throughout the country (not to mention two Emmys and a George Foster Peabody Award), was born in Pasadena, California, but has lived for many years in Cambridge, with her husband, Paul Child, a retired Foreign Service officer.

Sometime American ambassador to India, professor of economics emeritus at Harvard, full-time man of letters, Canadian-born JOHN KENNETH GALBRAITH brings to all his undertakings a degree of wit, style, and intellectual substance that dazzles. Galbraith is a resident of Cambridge, but can frequently be seen on the ski slopes of Gstaad, Switzerland, or shuttling between Boston, New York, and Washington.

JOSEPH E. GARLAND—whose father, Joseph, was a much-loved Boston pediatrician and editor of the celebrated *New England Journal of Medicine*—has written extensively on medical subjects. He is also the author of two books about the Gloucester fishery (*Lone Voyager* and *The Great Pattillo*) and of histories of Boston's North Shore and Gloucester's Eastern Point.

NANCY HALE has lived for many years in Charlottesville, Virginia, but her Boston roots run deep. She published her first book in 1932 and since then has written or edited some two dozen more, including novels, biographies, memoirs, and anthologies. Hale, who is married to the eminent English scholar Fredson Bowers, spends her summers in Gloucester.

Formerly a literary agent and publisher, LLEWELLYN HOWLAND III operates a rare-book business specializing in twentieth-century first editions and books relating to the sea. He is currently writing a history of American yachting.

JUSTIN KAPLAN, husband of Anne Bernays, is the author of *Mr. Clemens and Mark Twain*, *Lincoln Steffens*, and a forthcoming biography of Walt Whitman. He has taught at Harvard, has held a Guggenheim Fellowship, and has received a Pulitzer Prize in biography and a National Book Award in arts and letters.

JANE HOLTZ KAY is currently architecture and urban-design critic for *The Nation* and American correspondent for the British journal *Building Design*. Her work has also appeared in such diverse periodicals as *TV Guide*, *AIA Journal*, *Mademoiselle*, *Progressive Architecture*, and *Psychology Today*. Her book *Lost Boston* is being published this year. Kay lives in Brookline.

FELICIA LAMPORT was for some years a writer with M-G-M in Hollywood, and her acclaimed collections of light satirical verse, *Scrap Irony* and *Cultural Slag*, bespeak an intelligence honed by the study of the absurdities of American popular culture. An avid chess player, Lamport lives in Cambridge.

ALAN LUPO, born in the Mattapan district of Boston, is a leading practitioner of advocacy journalism; his understanding of the inner workings of Boston's neighborhoods is prodigious. A staff writer for the *Boston Phoenix*,

Lupo has published *Rites of Way* and *Liberty's Chosen Home* and is writing a third book with his wife, Caryl Rivers. They live in Winthrop.

ARCHIBALD MacLEISH, who introduces David McCord's contribution to this book, was awarded the Pulitzer Prize for poetry in 1953. A major American poet, essayist, and playwright, his other honors and achievements are too numerous to list.

A beloved figure in Boston literary circles, DAVID McCORD is the author or editor of countless books of poetry, and his verse has been included in more than 350 anthologies in the United States and abroad. A collection of his children's verse, *One at a Time*, was a recent National Book Award nominee. McCord is a Benjamin Franklin fellow of the Royal Society of Arts.

JAMES ALAN McPHERSON was born in Georgia and is a graduate of Morris Brown College and the Harvard Law School. His first collection of stories, *Hue and Cry*, was published in 1969; his second collection, *Elbow Room*, earned him the Pulitzer Prize for fiction in 1978. McPherson is a contributing editor of *The Atlantic Monthly*.

For many years a student of the private eye in American crime fiction—the subject of his doctoral dissertation—ROBERT B. PARKER then took to writing his own, highly successful series of detective novels (his fifth "Spencer" book, tentatively titled *Looking for Rachel Watson*, is due out shortly). Parker, a graduate of Colby College and a former Northeastern University English professor, lives in Lynnfield. In 1977 he won the Edgar Allan Poe Award of the Mystery Writers of America.

CARYL RIVERS, author of *Growing Up Catholic* and coauthor of the recent feminist work *Beyond Sugar and Spice*, shares with her husband, Alan Lupo, an abiding interest in Boston's neighborhoods and great skill as an advocacy journalist. Her work for women's rights is nationally recognized.

Born in Cambridge (her grandfather was a legendary superintendent of schools there), ELIZABETH (FITZGERALD) SAVAGE spent her high-school years in Missoula, Montana, but returned to New England to attend Colby College. Boston figures prominently in several of her ten novels, most obviously in the best-selling *The Last Night at the Ritz*. She and her husband, fellow-contributor Thomas Savage, live on the Maine coast.

THOMAS SAVAGE, husband of Elizabeth, was raised on a Montana sheep ranch. He was one of the earliest members of the English department at Brandeis University, and is perhaps best known for two novels, *Trust in Chariots* and *The Power of the Dog*. His novels *A Strange God* and *Daddy's Girl* are set largely in Boston and Boston's west suburbs. Savage was a 1979 Guggenheim Fellow.

JOHN D. SPOONER is "a stockbroker from nine to five, a writer all the time." Born in Brookline and a resident of Weston, Spooner has written four novels, including *The Pheasant-Lined Vest of Charlie Freeman* and *Class*, and two nonfiction works, *Confessions of a Stockbroker* and *Smart People*. Currently he is working on a screenplay.

ISABELLE STOREY, a native of Berne, Switzerland, came to the United States in 1958 and to Boston in 1973. She has been a curator of exhibitions at the Institute of Contemporary Art, and now organizes and designs exhibitions, principally in photography, on a freelance basis. Her shows have included "Lee Friedlander—The American Monument," "Marie Cosindas, 1960–1976" and "The Presence of Walker Evans." She lives on Beacon Hill with her husband, James Storey, a lawyer.

E. S. YNTEMA, a senior editor at the Atlantic Monthly Press, has worked closely with Julia Child on her two most recent cookbooks. Cooking and local history are two avocations easy and pleasant to pursue in Cambridge, where she lives with her husband and two daughters.

ACKNOWLEDGEMENTS

The picture editor for A BOOK FOR BOSTON was Isabelle Storey.

We gratefully acknowledge the following institutions and individuals who provided many of the photographs and illustrations in this book, and especially thank those who so generously gave of their time and expertise: Alfred A. Knopf, Inc.; Thomas Boylston Adams; Boston Athenaeum; Boston Public Library; Boston Red Sox; Boston Society of Architects; The Bostonian Society, Old State House; Copley Plaza Hotel; Francis A. Countway Library; Isabella Stewart Gardner Museum; Massachusetts General Hospital; Massachusetts Historical Society; Museum of Fine Arts, Boston; Society for the Preservation of New England Antiquities; Widener Library, Harvard University

A BOOK FOR BOSTON was composed by Arrow Composition, Inc., West Boylston, Massachusetts, in Linotype Electra, and was printed and bound by Halliday Lithograph Corporation, West Hanover and Plympton, Massachusetts, on International Paper's Bookmark, an entirely groundwood-free sheet, supplied by Carter Rice Storrs & Bement, Boston.

Electra is one of the few truly modern designs that has been widely adopted for book composition. It was designed by the incomparable William A. Dwiggins, who spent a good part of his prodigiously productive life in Hingham, Massachusetts. The typeface reflects his continued interest in the spirit of the twentieth century in its liveliness of line. The ornaments throughout the book are also of Dwiggins's invention, derived from his distinctive stencil designs for book decoration. The display type is Hermann Zapf's Melior, an excellent example of this master's ability to combine a calligraphic line with the technical demands of modern letter forms.

The book was designed in its entirety by Richard C. Bartlett, whose dedication and taste are herewith acknowledged with great gratitude. Ann Hatfield provided assistance with the layouts and prepared the mechanicals. The copyeditor was Hilary Horton, and the proofreaders were Geraldine C. Morse and Suzanna Kaysen. The production was coordinated by Kathleen Riley.